Time

KEY CONCEPTS

Published

Barbara Adam, *Time*
Alan Aldridge, *Consumption*
Colin Barnes and Geof Mercer, *Disability*
Mildred Blaxter, *Health*
Steve Bruce, *Fundamentalism*
Anthony Elliott, *Concepts of the Self*
Steve Fenton, *Ethnicity*
Michael Freeman, *Human Rights*
Michael Saward, *Democracy*
John Scott, *Power*
Anthony D. Smith, *Nationalism*

Time

Barbara Adam

polity

First published in 2004 by Polity Press Ltd.

Polity Press
65 Bridge Street
Cambridge CB2 1UR, UK

Polity Press
350 Main Street
Malden, MA 02148, USA

A catalogue record for this book is available from the British Library.

Library of Congress Cataloging-in-Publication Data
Adam, Barbara, 1945–
    Time / Barbara Adam.
        p.   cm. –
    ISBN 0-7456-2777-3 (hc : acid-free) – ISBN 0-7456-2778-1 (pb : acid-free)
    1. Time – Sociological aspects.   2. Time – Social aspects.
I. Title.   II. Series: Key concepts (Polity Press)
    HM656A33 2004
    304.2'3 – dc22   2003015021

Typeset in 10.5 on 12 pt Sabon
by SNP Best-set Typesetter Ltd., Hong Kong
Printed and bound in Great Britain by
MPG Books, Bodmin, Cornwall

For further information on Polity, visit our website:
www.polity.co.uk

Contents

Acknowledgements   viii

Prologue   1

PART I   What is Time?   3

Interlude: Time Is   5

1   **Time Stories**   6
    Gods of Time   6
    In the Beginning   8
    Paradise and the Fall   11
    Encounters with Death   12
    Journeys to the Otherworld   13
    Cycles of Renewal and Regeneration   14
    Beyond Death: Resurrection and Redemption   16
    Reflections: Myth for Today's Theory and Practice   17

    Interlude: Representations of Time   21

2   **Time Theories I**   22
    Western Philosophy: Ontology to Epistemology   23
    Natural Science: Clockwork Universe and Change   29
    Enlightenment Theories: *A Priori* and Dialectic   33
    Social Theory: Practice, Value and Category   36

    Interlude: Time Perspectives   50

3 Time Theories II   51
   Western Philosophy: Time Within   51
   The Sciences of System-Specific Times   60
   Social Theory and the Past, Present and Future   64

PART II What is the Role of Time in Social Life? 71

   Interlude: Time Transcendence   74

4 **Cultural Practices of Time Transcendence**   75
   Making Time Stand Still   76
   Knowing Fate, Forging Futures   82
   Creating Immortality and Permanence   89
   Modifying Nature's Times and Rhythms   94
   Superimposing Phases and Social Structure   98

   Interlude: Body Time, Clock Time, Social Time 101

5 **In Pursuit of Time Know-how**   102
   Reckoning Time   103
   Creating Clock Time   112
   Mobilizing World Time   117
   Networking Instantaneity   119

   Interlude: Time Complexities & Hierarchies   122

6 **The Quest for Time Control**   123
   Commodification   124
   Compressions   128
   Colonization   136
   Control   143

   Interlude: Futures   149

Epilogue   150

Notes   153
Further Reading   166
Bibliography   168
Index   177

To †Michael Young

Inspirational Time Lord
Mentor, colleague & friend
Whose wisdom & acute observations
At our Dartington meetings
Will be deeply missed

Acknowledgements

I would like to extend a heartfelt thank you to my colleagues and students Stuart Allan, Judy Amstrong, Helen Broutchert, Catherine Butler, Mahmoud Ezzamel, Ronald Frankenberg, Maggie Gregory, Peter Harris, Robert Hassan, Martin Held, William Housley, Gabrielle Ivinson, Tom Keenoy, Jamie Lewis, John Roberts, Peter Samuels, Paul White and Elden Wiebe for reading the draft of this text. Their enthusiasm was hugely encouraging and their helpful comments gave plenty of food for thought. Wherever possible, their perceptive recommendations for change were incorporated in the final version of this book. My special thanks go to my husband, Jan, for his sustained support and constructive criticism, to my daughter, Miriam, who once more has checked my references with great diligence, and to my grandchildren, wider family and friends for their tolerance of my extended absences from social activities in the evenings and on weekends.

Prologue

In this book I want to take you on a journey of seeing time through many different lenses. Through myth and stories, theories ancient and modern, ritual and daily interactions, institutions and power relations I attempt to open up the sociocultural world in its temporal diversity. I am not concerned to adjudicate between the kaleidoscope of different views and perspectives. Instead, the idea is to show the diversity in practice and demonstrate how many so-called incompatible perspectives sit comfortably side by side while others can be held simultaneously without causing cognitive dissonance or distress. Thus an account of layers of meaning rather than Truth in the singular is attempted in these pages: a rich landscape for the reader to wander and stroll in, an occasional maze to feel lost in.

Time is lived, experienced, known, theorized, created, regulated, sold and controlled. It is contextual and historical, embodied and objectified, abstracted and constructed, represented and commodified. In these multiple expressions time is an inescapable fact of social life and cultural existence. In this introductory text, therefore, I can do no more than open a window on this subject and give you pointers to sources that can help to deepen your understanding of this inexhaustibly fascinating field of enquiry. Towards this end I draw on the work of archaeologists and archaeoastronomers, anthropologists and architects, empirical sociologists and

geographers, historians and religious scholars, literary theorists and social psychologists, mathematicians and philosophers. This particular constellation of sources coupled with
my own intellectual base in social theory colours what I find
interesting and worthy of discussion, what stories I tell and
which ones I leave out.

Moreover, given the pervasiveness of time in the history of
human cultures, any selection of approaches to time is of
necessity highly arbitrary. I therefore focus on some of the
beacons as they appear from my particular biographical
present. In light of the enormity and wealth of recorded
thought on the matter, it could not be otherwise. It is thus
my particular torchlight on the subject matter that illuminates
some thoughts for discussion, identifies some as worthy of
mention and others, though no less important in the historical scheme of things, as insignificant or irrelevant to the story
I want to tell in these pages.

Theories by themselves, I want to propose, are not sufficient
for understanding time as a key concept. Instead there is an
additional need to ground knowledge of the social relations of
time in particular practices and technologies. This entails that
we recognize time as theory and practice, experience and
explanation, lived orientation and material expression. Consequently the conceptual journey embarked on in this book
takes us into the realms of embodied knowledge, theory-
impregnated practices and technologies as praxis, that is, as
expressive of theory, practice and implicit understanding in
action.

The time worlds encountered in the course of this journey
differ greatly with regard to both their content and form. In
sympathy with these differences, the stories I tell change form
in accordance with their respective subjects. Thus the pithy
form of ancient myths and religious texts is replicated in the
stories of time that constitute the book's beginning, the interdependent complexity of contemporary temporal relations
reflected in the way the story is brought to an end.

The short 'interludes' between chapters offer an alternative window on the temporalities in question. They present
in compressed form the diversity of temporalities addressed
in and across the chapters. Their poetic shapes not only
express but underline the constructed nature of the subject
matter under discussion.

Part I
What is Time?

Time is about God and the universe and all things human. Time is everywhere and it permeates everything: the cosmos, our solar system, the earth's past, present and future, socio-cultural existence. As such it has suffused knowledge since the dawn of humanity. It has occupied such a central place in the history of ideas and cultural practice because the temporality of being confronts us with the immemorial, existential issues of life and death, origin and destiny. What then is time? We know that the clock tells us *the* time, but it does not tell us what time *is*. We live time, we experience it daily as an integral part of existence. We know it intimately and yet the answer to this simple question seems extraordinarily difficult.

Questions about the nature of time have occupied thinkers for thousands of years. Few of them, however, have achieved consensus on their answers. In fact, as you will see, their conceptualizations of time are as varied as the theories of nature and culture, the perspectives on society and the belief systems that have existed across the ages. Today these ancient beliefs and understandings of time form the bedrock of tacit knowledge on which we conduct our daily lives as children and parents, teachers and students. Even social scientists charged with the explanation of social life tend to take time for granted, leaving it unaddressed as an implicated rather than explicated feature of their theories and empirical studies.

Some notable exceptions to this norm are discussed in these pages.

In part I of this book I explore some of the most significant answers to the question, 'What is time?' Here our journey takes us to knowledge practices shared by many cultures: to prehistoric myths and rituals, ancient stories and theories concerned with human origin and destiny. Along the way we meander through the philosophical theories of ancient Greece and the Middle East, religious thought from the Middle Ages and Enlightenment philosophies, and finally theories of the industrial age, which we consider in a bit more detail.

The book begins with collective representations of archaic knowledge. In 'Time Stories', the question 'What is time?' is addressed in the form most suited to the subject matter. It is told as myths and stories so that form and content may cohere as an integrated whole. The structure of this first chapter moves from a time embodied in deities to time as the creation of God or gods. It identifies the progression from a period of atemporal bliss to one of toil in finite existence and from paradise lost to anticipated redemption. Pivotal to this first chapter is the encounter with finitude and change, a theme that is central to this book and will be revisited most explicitly in chapter 4 where practices of time transcendence are investigated.

Time stories are followed by time theories, oral by written accounts, holistic collective representations by more focused and detailed thoughts attributed to individual thinkers. Chapters 2 and 3 trace the development of time theory from Greek philosophy to the founders of social theory. The enormous wealth of material covered in 'time theories' has made some kind of division essential. As with all categorizations the line of partition is somewhat arbitrary, with some theorists fitting their respective allocations better than others. Irrespective of the specific distinctions between approaches to time, however, in this book theories are treated as stories by alternative means – emanating from identifiable named sources and directed at a more select audience, but stories nevertheless. The narrative form therefore changes in accordance with the particular account of time theories presented here.

INTERLUDE

TIME IS

Time Is
Time is order
Time is endurance
Time is stability and structure
Time is persistence and permanence
Time is repetition, cyclicality, rhythmicity
Time is beginning and end, pause and transition
Time is difference between before & after, cause & effect
Time is life & death, growth & decay, night & day
Time is change, transience and ephemerality
Time is evolution, history, development
Time is flux and transformation
Time is process & potential
Time is mutability
Time is chaos
Time Is
Time is speed
Time is duration
Time is simultaneity
Time is Chronos & Kairos
Time is past, present & future
Time is the succession of moments
Time is memory, perception & anticipation
Time is commodity & exchange value
Time is the measure of motion
Time is *a priori* intuition
Time is instantaneity
Time is a resource
Time is money
Time is gift
Time Is
Time is flying
Time is passing
Time is continuing
Time is marching on
Time is waiting for no one
Time is vanishing like a dream
Time is going on forever
Time is evaporating
Time is becoming
Time is times
Time Is

1
Time Stories

Gods of Time

Sun and Moon

Re, Egyptian sun god and ruler of time, changed his shape with every hour of the day, making visible the repeating processes of the sun's cycle: rising as a scarab, descending into the darkness of the otherworld as a crocodile and re-emerging at dawn in the form of a double lion.[1]

Sūrya, sun god of India, rides through the skies on his chariot. He resides at the centre of creation between the manifest and invisible worlds. As maker of the day and eternity he is the supreme soul, spirit and source of time.[2]

In China the sun god, Shen Yi, and the moon god, Heng E, are husband and wife; as yang and yin they symbolize the two complementary forces of the universe. Their daily tasks concern the eternal ordering of time. On every fifteenth day after a New Moon Shen Yi visits Heng E, giving the full moon its bright glow.[3]

Tarqeq, the Inuit moon spirit, is responsible for fertility and propriety and controls the patterns of animal migration.[4]

Sky and Underworld

Every evening at nightfall, Nut, the Egyptian goddess of the sky, devours the sun god Re, the creator and complete one, and every morning she gives birth to him. She is the mother, the source of death and resurrection, home of the dead from which new life springs forth.[5]

Light and Energy

Aion, Greek god of time and eternity, is lord of light and dark, all-embracing spirit and gatekeeper of the realm beyond. Originally the source of all living beings' vital fluid, Aion is energy, the dynamic aspect of existence and the lifespan.[6]

India's Lord Shiva is called 'great time' and 'all-devouring time'; he embodies universal energy, both active and destructive. In his threefold form he is Brahma the creator, Vishnu the sustainer and Kalaruda the destroyer. Kali, goddess of destruction and all-pervasive power of time, is a further aspect of Shiva. She is the destroyer who activates the creative powers of Shiva. Through his dance Shiva awakens inert matter, animates the inanimate world and brings forth the cycles of time: birth and death, creation and destruction.[7]

Fire and Water

Omotéotl, Aztec creator god, lord of fire and lord of time, is mother and father of everything, provider and supporter of all life on earth. He is the light that illuminates things and the mirror that reflects all being.[8]

The Celtic goddess Nantosuelta, whose name means 'stream', is one of two sources of life. The other is Sucellos, the striker, god of solar power who softens and thaws the earth to bring forth life. In the interplay between sun/fire and water, the two primary sources of life, the rhythm of the seasons is created.[9]

In Egyptian Heliopolitan cosmology, Nu or Nun is god of the primordial water, the wild undifferentiated chaos from which the sun god and all life emerged.[10]

Oceanos-Chronos, Greek god of the primary substance and the eternal river of time, controls all change. He is creator and destroyer of everything. As water Oceanos encircles the world, forms its boundary and is the origin of all things.[11]

Deities of Magic Moments

Nike, Greek goddess of victory, represents the pivotal point on the scales, the magical moment when a game or battle turns to victory. Nike appears and disappears suddenly.

Kairos, Greek god of lucky coincidence and the right moment for favourable action, has to be grasped firmly or he escapes and the magical moment is irrevocably gone.

Fortuna, Roman goddess of good or bad luck, bestows fortune blindly, not taking account of whether or not the recipients of her attention deserve what she has in stall for them.[12]

In the Beginning

In the creation myth of ancient Persia, finite time begins with the rule of Ohrmazd, the all-powerful good spirit. Finite time emerged from and was created by infinite time.

> Except Time all things are created. Time is the creator; and Time has no limit, neither top nor bottom. It has always been and shall be for evermore. No sensible person will say whence Time has come. In spite of all the grandeur that surrounded it, there was no one to call it creator; for it had not brought forth creation. It then created fire and water; and when it had brought them together, Ohrmazd came into existence, and simultaneously Time became Creator and Lord with regard to the creation it had brought forth.[13]

Enûma Eliš, the creation myth of ancient Mesopotamia, tells of a struggle between the principal deity, Marduk, and the water goddess Tiamat. Marduk's eventual victory brings to an end chaos and anarchy. From the fragments of Tiamat's torn body Marduk creates the cosmos and from the blood of the demon Kingu he forms the first humans. To ensure the continued maintenance of order over chaos, every New

Year this battle between the primordial forces has to be re-enacted.[14]

In Maori mythology, 'Io dwelt within the breathing space of immensity. The universe was in darkness with water everywhere; there was no glimmer of dawn, no clearness, no light . . . And he [Io] began by saying these words: "Let there be light into Tawhito, a dominion of light, a bright light." Darkness became a light-possessing darkness and at once light appeared. Now a great light prevailed.'[15]

Australian Aborigines depict their beginning in the following way: 'Once the earth was completely dark and silent. Nothing moved upon its barren face . . . Inside a deep cave below the Nullarbor plane slept a beautiful woman, the Sun. The Great Father Spirit gently woke her and told her to emerge from the cave and stir the universe into life.'[16] This took place in Altyerrenge, 'dream time' [and space],[17] the realm of the great Spirit Ancestors who formed all beings from the same life essence, creating a network of kinship that encompasses the non-human and the non-empirical world, past, present and future. After the creation of humans the Spirit Ancestors retired to Altyerrenge from where they continue their engagement with the daily life of humans and related creatures. The souls of all newborns come from that realm and the dead return to it.[18]

Geronimo tells the story of Apache origin thus:

> In the beginning there was darkness on the earth. At that time 'all creatures had the power of speech and were gifted with reason'. The bird led by the eagle wished to admit light into the darkness but the beasts led by a nameless monster wished the darkness to remain. There was a great battle when the eagle dropped an enormous stone upon the monster. Then the light came into darkness. Man too had a part in the struggle. A boy killed with arrows a dragon that had been devouring the children of men in the darkness, and the boy became the father of Geronimo's people.[19]

In Icelandic mythology the world was created by the interplay between fire and ice. 'In the beginning, so the story tells, there was neither land nor sea nor sky, only a vast chasm of emptiness called Ginnungapap.' North of Ginnungapap there formed plumes of freezing mist that turned into the land of ice, and south of Ginnungapap flames danced on the blackness to form an 'all-consuming sea of fire'.

> Fire melts ice and ice quenches fire, and in the middle of Ginnungapap was a place that was neither biting cold nor searing hot but mild and gentle as a summer's day. Here warm breezes from the south caressed the ice from the north as a minstrel strokes the strings of his harp, and under their soft touch the ice began to yield its hardness and to melt, and in the first trickling drops of melted ice the seeds of life stirred.[20]

In the Book of Genesis (1: 1–6), the first day of creation is described in these words:

> In the beginning God created the heavens and the earth. The earth was without form, and void, and darkness was upon the face of the deep; and the Spirit of God was moving over the face of the waters.
> And God said, 'Let there be light'; and there was light. And God saw that the light was good; and God separated the light from the darkness. God called the light Day, and the darkness he called Night. And there was evening and there was morning, one day.[21]

The New Testament, in the Prologue to the Gospel According to John, relates a different beginning, an origin tied to *logos,* the eternal principle and universal agent of creation which is conceived as unifying logic, the word and God.

> In the beginning was the Word:
> the Word was with God
> and the Word was God
> He was with God in the beginning.
> Through him all things came into being,
> not one thing came into being except through him.
> What has come into being in him was life,
> life that was in the light of men;
> and light shines in darkness,
> and darkness would not overpower it.[22]

In the scientific age of the twentieth century, physicists informed us that the universe emerged with the 'big bang',

an explosion of intense heat and light. With this first split-
ting of a primeval atom, some physicists suggest, the universe
began to differentiate and expand. 'Ever since the beginning,
gravity has been amplifying inhomogeneities, building up
structures, and enhancing temperature contrasts – a pre-
requisite for the emergence of the complexity that lies before
us and of which we are part.'[23]

Paradise and the Fall

In the beginning, before time began, humans lived a life of
plenty, a life in which they knew neither suffering nor toil.
This state or realm was variously called 'paradise', 'Dreaming' or the 'Garden of Eden'. Ageing, illness and death had
not yet entered human existence. People walked freely and
without fear among the wild beasts. It was a time of spiritual
and material plenitude, a world radiant with light and beauty.
The air was filled with heavenly scent and music. In this realm
the parent God/gods mingled with innocent, childlike earth-
lings. The separating boundary between heaven and earth
had not yet been drawn.[24]

This blissful existence before and outside time was tied to
certain conditions laid down by God/gods. As long as these
preconditions – often in the form of rules and commandments
– were adhered to, continuity of the carefree life in paradise
was ensured for all.[25] It was the deliberate or accidental
actions of humans – eating from the tree of knowledge, dis-
obeying the rules, annoying God/gods, cutting vital links – that
brought to an end the state of paradise. Separation has taken
two forms: the withdrawal of God/gods from the earthly
paradise to inaccessible parts of heaven, and the banishment
of humans from the realm of innocence before time.

The consequences of the fall have been devastating. Heavenly bliss and the cornucopia were replaced by fear and toil,
atemporal being by temporality and finitude, growth and
decay. Eternal spring gave way to seasonal variation, immortal existence to earthly being, to birth and death, ageing and
disease. Mortality and finitude became a feature of life – faced
and feared; the hero's death revered. The battle with time
commenced.

Encounters with Death

In Norse mythology the gods of Asgard retained their eternal youth by eating the golden apples supplied by Idun, keeper of the apples of immortality. When Loki betrayed Idun and delivered her to the giant, Thjazi, who imprisoned her in a fortress in the land beyond the rainbow, the gods lost their protection against the ravages of time. Faced with their rapid disintegration, Odin forced Loki to rescue Idun from captivity in the land of giants. On Idun's safe return, 'the gods reached into the basket and took of the apples, and they ate, and they ate and they ate . . .'[26]

In the epic of Gilgamesh[27] the ruler of a small Assyrian kingdom found in Enkidu another man he could respect. Gilgamesh and Enkidu became close friends and went on many adventures together, slaying monsters that had plagued the forest and threatened the city. One day the goddess of the city asked Gilgamesh to make love to her. Knowing that this would bring forth his death, he refused. His life was saved but that of his friend was taken instead. Enkidu became sick and died. Confronted with his friend's death, Gilgamesh lamented:

> Enkidu, I weep for you like a wailing woman. You were the axe by my side, the sword in my belt, the shield before me. I will also die and worms will feast on my flesh. I now fear death and have lost all my courage.[28]

Through his friend's death Gilgamesh was faced with his own mortality. Deeply unsettled by that knowledge, he sets out on a quest for eternal life. He searches across all time and space, encountering beings from the distant past and faraway places, only to find that humans cannot achieve everlasting life for themselves, that immortality is a gift of the gods. The journey has tempered Gilgamesh's spirit, endowed him with wisdom. At the end of his quest Gilgamesh knew that there was no permanence, that all things must pass, that everything has its time and season.

Osiris, god-king of ancient Egypt, who reigned at a time of peace and justice, was murdered by his jealous brother

Seth, who dismembered him and dispersed Osiris's body parts across the entire kingdom. These were discovered and gathered up by Isis, wife and sister of Osiris. Together with Nephthys, her sister, and with the additional help of numerous gods, Isis was able to reassemble Osiris's body, wrap him in his own skin and reanimate him. With the natural order restored and his integrity re-established, Osiris was able to rise again and take his rightful place in the land of immortals as Lord of the Dead.[29]

Journeys to the Otherworld

The story told by Homer in the *Odyssey* is of a quest not for immortality but for the safe return to mortal existence after extensive encounters with the deaths of friends and foes during the long war against Troy.[30] On the perilous journey home, which lasted a full ten years, Odysseus encountered many dangers and temptations. He met lotus-eaters, a Cyclops, the master of winds, cannibals, an enchantress, the ghosts of the dead, sirens, sea monsters and a goddess. For Odysseus death was not only a danger but also a lure. As he was drawn into the beauty and ease of life in the otherworld of witches, sirens and goddesses, so the life and wife that he sought to return to receded further and further into the distance, faded into the shadow, became less real. 'To break the spell of death he must embrace finite existence.'[31] He had to choose life and love as a mortal over death and love as an immortal.

Dante's story in the *Divine Comedy* is one not of deeds but of experience, of an encounter with the immortal spirit.[32] One day, in the middle of his life, Dante found himself lost in a forest, meeting a leopard, a lion and a wolf. The immortal spirit of the Roman poet Virgil offered to guide him home. The path however was to lead through the realms of hell, purgatory and heaven. Dante followed reluctantly through the gateway that told him to abandon all hope. In hell he found the spirits of the driven and obsessed, those whose lives had been full of violence and fraud. Their punishment was that they were unable to die and thus had no hope of achieving final peace. Their anguished state was eternal, without time.

In the story purgatory was a large mountain with seven stations, one for each of the seven deadly sins, which had to be conquered. Hope re-emerged because in the realm of purgatory actions have consequences. This meant that time, the passage of time, became of the utmost importance. Virgil encouraged Dante to hurry, scolded him for lingering and reminded him that today never comes again, that the time appointed to us must be put to better use. Souls, he explained to Dante, find themselves in the realm of purgatory not just for past bad deeds but also for missed opportunities. In life you cannot attain fame with a careless attitude to time. You cannot achieve a status that will outlast you if you do not use your allotted time to best advantage:

> 'Now must thou thus cast off all sloth,' said the master, 'for sitting down or under blankets none comes to fame, and without it he that consumes his life leaves such trace of himself as smoke in air or foam on water.'[33]

As Dante climbed higher and higher he became ever lighter, delivered from the weight of the deadly sins and associated cravings. At the summit of the mountain of purgatory Dante was so light that he could ascend into heaven. From this point onwards, not Virgil but Beatrice became his guide. Her presence marked the turning point between his old and new spirit life. With Beatrice at his side, Dante was fired by the eternal, timeless 'love that moves the sun and the other stars'.[34]

Cycles of Renewal and Regeneration

An Aztec myth tells of the battle between sun and moon. According to this story, in the beginning there was only the moon and her four hundred brothers, the stars, all of them children of the mother goddess, Coatlicu. Coatlicu was murdered by her children for bringing shame to the family of gods, by being impregnated by an unknown force. The child of this union was the sun, who avenged the death of his mother in a fierce battle with the gods of the night. The sun was victorious and transformed night into day. This drama is re-enacted daily, with the sun 'shooting his arrows of light into the night sky and banishing the darkness'.[35]

The Babylonian goddess Ishtar, queen of the sky, went in search of the spirit of her beloved Tammuz, god of vegetation and corn, who was cruelly murdered. On her journey to the realm of dead souls and land of no return, which was ruled by her sister Erishkigal, Ishtar faced many perils and torments. While Ishtar was imprisoned in the netherworld, nothing could grow and flourish on earth. The desolation on earth became so great that the gods pleaded with Sîn, 'lord of magic and master of the waters that nourish the world and contain all wisdom', to intervene. A deal was struck that restored Ishtar to her former power and beauty and allowed Tammuz to return to the living. There was, however, one condition: Tammuz could only spend half the year in freedom, and the other half had to be spent with Ishtar's sister in the otherworld.

> When Tammuz was with Ishtar on the earth, the goddess rejoiced and nature and man flourished. But when he returned to Erishkigal below, Ishtar grieved and all signs of life died.
> This is how it has been from the beginning of time and this is how it will be to the end.[36]

A very similar explanation for the seasons is given in Greek mythology. Pluto, King of the Underworld, abducted Persephone, daughter of Demeter and Zeus, to be his queen in the shadowy dark of his kingdom. Many a day the distraught Demeter wandered across land and sea in search of her beloved daughter, until one day a nymph was able to tell her of Persephone's fate. In her anguish, Demeter, the goddess of fruitfulness, cursed the earth. Her tears fell as plague on fields and beasts. People wasted away in the ensuing famine. To bring the devastation to an end Zeus gave a ruling that should appease both his brother and his wife. He decreed that Persephone would spend half the year with Pluto and the other half with her mother. Joyful was Demeter and glad was the earth of her joy: the scorched earth and withered trees blossomed, mountains were again clothed in green, the fields bore fruit and all was well. But every year darkness and barrenness returned when Persephone rejoined Pluto in the shadowlands of Hades, until, in spring, she was returned to her mother's arms and the earth began to breathe again.[37]

In Indian mythology, the universe is recreated in ongoing cycles of creation and destruction that have no beginning and no end. The story of the 'Churning of the Ocean of Milk'[38] explains what had happened when at the beginning of the second cycle certain elements were still missing, the most important of which was amrita, the sacred butter, source of the gods' supremacy. To obtain the amrita the gods had to churn the great ocean of milk until it turned to butter. Clearly this was a task they could not complete on their own. They had to call on the help of their enemies, the demons. With the promise that they would share this source of their power in exchange for the demons' assistance they were able to set to the task. They uprooted Mount Mandara and used Vâsuki, King of the Serpents, as their rope. After one thousand years of turning the mountain, the coveted missing treasures began to emerge from the ocean of milk: the Sacred Cow, 'wetnurse of everything living', the Goddess of Wine, the perfumed Tree of Paradise, the Nymphs of Beauty and Grace, and last but not least the amrita. The plan of the demons to steal the amrita for themselves was foiled and the supremacy of the gods over creation was restored.

Beyond Death: Resurrection and Redemption

In the Christian stories of the life of Jesus as told in the Gospels of Matthew, Mark, Luke and John, Jesus dies on the cross and rises from the dead. Jesus bids his disciples to remember that he will be with them 'always, to the close of the age'.[39] Jesus's second coming is told in the Book of Revelation. Three times John records the words of God: 'I am the Alpha and the Omega.'

> In his presence earth and sky vanished, leaving no trace . . .
> The sea gave up all the dead who were in it; Death and Hades were emptied of the dead that were in them; and everyone was judged as his deeds deserved.

Then death and Hades were hurled into the burning lake. This burning lake is the second death; and anyone whose name could not be found written in the book of life was hurled into the burning lake.

Then I saw a *new heaven and a new earth* . . .

I saw the holy city, the new Jerusalem coming down out of heaven from God . . .

Then the One sitting on the throne spoke: Look. I am making the whole of creation new . . .

.   .   .

The curse of destruction will be abolished . . .

And night will be abolished; they will not need lamp-light or sunlight, because Lord God will be shining on them . . .

.   .   .

I am the Alpha and the Omega, *the First and the Last*, the Beginning and the End.[40]

Reflections: Myth for Today's Theory and Practice

Why start a book on time with mythological stories about origin and destiny? What could we possibly hope to glean from ancient predecessors' preoccupations with death and their concern with the otherworld? What relevance could stories about gods, paradise and mythical heroes have for understanding our own contemporary condition, for comprehending the nature of our lives of schedules, deadlines and time pressure?

As the chapters in this book will show, the pertinence of these mythical tales is manifold. The stories confront us with aspects of time and the temporality of being that have tended to slip out of sight with the industrial way of life. They bring to the fore concerns with origin and destiny, with the meaning of human being and the role of time for human existence. They address matters concerning the finality and contingency of being and non-being and consider the place and role of humans in the cosmic scheme of things. They acknowledge that transience and finitude place limits on human being, define it as less than perfect, create fears and anxieties. The stories and myths explain the earth-bound condition and its transcendence, give answers to questions about who we are, define the purpose and meaning of our being in the world. With respect to those primary questions about existence, these ancient stories have lost none of their pertinence over the hundreds and thousands of years of their retelling. Moreover, they give us vital clues about the origin and nature of human culture.

Thus, with the deification of time, archaic cultures have acknowledged the key role of time for all existence. Through their gods they have identified time with the sun and moon, with light and energy, fire and water. They have recognized that time permeates everything and have acknowledged its importance for the creation and destruction of life, for birth and death, growth and decay. The mythological stories operate simultaneously at three different temporal levels: the human level, which includes both individuals and society, the cosmic level of stars, planets and the universe, and the spiritual level which encompasses the otherworld of deities and dead spirits, heaven and hell, paradise and nirvana. It is the human level which is the most explicitly bound by the finitude of earthly time. The cosmic level is marked by cycles of eternal return and renewal, while the spiritual level is beyond time – it precedes and transcends earthly time. Meaningful life, the myths suggest, is one that is integrated into these three realms of being and that manages to connect the associated times of existence. In mythical stories the finitude of human life is therefore related to the never-ending cycles of the cosmos as well as the eternal realm of God/gods and the spirits of the dead.

In mythology individual birth and death are related to collective beginning and end, origin and destiny. Individual birth, the change from a safe environment to the painful expulsion into an uncertain world, is paralleled by the collective loss of paradise and the beginning of earthly human existence. Since death cannot be lived through, that is, since death is outside the realm of experience, knowledge about the end of life is often sought in its beginning. Across the ages in most cultures creation myths tell of a blissful timeless existence followed by the fall from grace and with it the beginning of time. Death emergences with the expulsion from paradise, just as the process of dying begins with birth. Human being, time, birth and death become inextricably intertwined.

To escape the 'curse of time' and the terror of non-existence, of nothingness after death, people have chosen different solutions to the existential dilemma. The spirit of the dead returns from whence it came, back to the realm of Dreaming, for example. Alternatively, it emulates the planetary path of eternal return; is resurrected or reincarnated; or goes before a heavenly court to be judged worthy of ascent to heaven or to be condemned to hell. The first solution is marked by an effort to return to hallowed origins; the second by integration into the cosmic scheme of things, with eventual deliverance to the spiritual realm; and the third by progression towards a future state, the nature of which is dependent on actions during one's lifetime. No matter how the afterlife is conceived, it seems that meaningful existence is tied to the belief that life does not end with death. This entails finding a relationship to that which cannot be experienced and encompassed.

The mythological quest for eternal life therefore becomes a quest for knowledge: knowledge about death and about what lies beyond. Only the spirit,[41] however, can probe the realms beyond time. Only the spirit is free to explore the world beyond death and thus able to provide a guide to deeper existence and enlightenment. However, some advances in this spiritual quest, it seems, have been accompanied by an inescapable distancing from nature and an ever-widening gap between body and spirit, earth and otherworld, between human life in finite time and spirit existence in an atemporal, eternal realm. This separation laid the foundation for later philosophical theories of Greek antiquity in which Plato posited two separate realms: the one covering phenomena, that is, things extended in time and space that are subject to change; the other encompassing *noumena*, eternal ideas as the form or essence of phenomena that fall outside the temporal realm of earthly being. The distancing of human being from nature, brought about by the foreknowledge of death and the quest for immortality, moreover, facilitated sociocultural activity as a means to transcend the earthly condition. One of its cultural products, the natural science of our own age, was in turn to locate immortality in the body with the theory that genes ensure individual immortality.[42]

Culture arises with the relationship to finitude as inescapable human condition, for 'death', as Reanney points out, 'is the midwife of creative change, of transcendence'.[43] Through cultural activity people create a world that endures beyond their personal lifespans, a world that renders mortal being immortal. Thus Dante's story and the legends of classical heroes press the importance of fame as that which outlasts a person and makes their life worthy of being preserved in legends and folk tales. As I show in chapter 4, pyramids and cave art, myth and writing, ritual and religion are all cultural means to transcend individual being beyond its allotted earthly time. All are responses to the inevitability of finitude. To understand the temporality of contemporary life, therefore, takes us not only on an exploration of time in theory and practice but also on a deeper quest for knowledge about the temporality of human being.

INTERLUDE

REPRESENTATIONS OF TIME

Cycle
The time of the cycle is process
The time of the cycle is rhythmicity
The time of the cycle is life and death
The time of the cycle is cosmic creativity
The time of the cycle is change-continuum
The time of the cycle is sequence and duration
The time of the cycle is repetition of the similar
The time of the cycle is intersecting before and after
The time of the cycle is bounded by observers' timeframes
The time of the cycle is past & future expressed in the living present

Spiral
The time of the spiral is Tao
The time of the spiral is dynamic
The time of the spiral is a journey
The time of the spiral is development
The time of the spiral is symbol of eternity
The time of the spiral is projection and destiny
The time of the spiral is encoded pasts and futures
The time of the spiral is binding duration and progression
The time of the spiral is yin & yang, immanence & transcendence

Circle
The time of the circle is stability
The time of the circle is timelessness
The time of the circle is created eternity
The time of the circle is repetition of the same
The time of the circle is duration and endurance
The time of the circle is past & future in the present
The time of the circle is memory, ritual and anticipation
The time of the circle is extending the now to origin & destiny

Point
The time of the point is origin
The time of the point is stillness
The time of the point is eternal now
The time of the point is the vertical axis
The time of the point is the beginning & end
The time of the point is unifying the one and all
The time of the point is indivisible, atomic & absolute

Line
The time of the line is spatial
The time of the line is historical
The time of the line is projective
The time of the line is irreversible
The time of the line is before & after
The time of the line is tied to a beginning

2
Time Theories I

We have no problem recognizing time in the second interlude's symbolic representations. We can acknowledge their truth value, despite the fact that not all of them can be focused on simultaneously and not every aspect is compatible with every other. In our everyday lives we weave in and out of this diversity of features without giving much thought to the matter. Without problem, we navigate through the inherent contradictions, knowing them as integral parts of the wider whole that constitutes time. In our social theories, in contrast, we seem to home in on certain aspects in preference to others, come down on the side of one pair of opposites, or choose one duality at the expense of all others.

There has been much discussion about the neglect of time in social theory but when we look more closely it becomes apparent that the founders of the social sciences have been concerned to encompass time in their respective theories. Thus Marx, Weber, Durkheim, Mead and Schutz have given attention to this most difficult of subjects. It almost seems as if any new perspective on social life (and the material and living world, for that matter) required an engagement with time. Or to put it differently, any new perspective on the world entails a reconceptualization of the temporal relations involved. In Western traditions of thought this engagement with time can be traced back to Greek philosophy of the sixth century BC and beyond to the ancient civilizations of Egypt, Mesopotamia and Assyria.

To steer through and explain the philosophical theories of time is a daunting task for any expert in the field; for an amateur it would be a foolhardy enterprise. And yet there is clear evidence that the founders of social science not only drew on that intellectual heritage but actively engaged with it in the process of establishing new social science perspectives. Thus, while it is not my intention to offer detailed analyses of the many varied philosophical approaches to time, I do want to provide outlines of some of the key positions that underpin contemporary explorations in social time by Western social theorists.

Both the choice of philosophers and the selection from their lifetime's work was guided by what I considered most relevant as background knowledge to the contemporary social theories discussed in this extended essay on time as a key concept. The very distinct contemporary perspectives on social time prompted me to trace their respective conceptual histories back to the classical theories of Greece and beyond and to distinguish the theory traditions roughly along the absolute/objective to relative/subjective axis that divides the approaches to time of the founders of social science. Clearly, not every thinker fits equally well into the imposed categorization. The eighteenth-century philosopher G. W. F. Hegel in particular sits most uncomfortably in his allocated chapter. Such anomalies, however, should not worry us unduly as long as we remain aware of the constructed and pragmatic nature of the divide.

Western Philosophy: Ontology to Epistemology

Early Greek philosophers were concerned to understand the relations between persistent Being and changing beings, between permanence and ephemerality, mortality and immortality.[1] In their philosophies of nature they considered how persistence, transience and motion were possible. They asked about the ontological status of time: is it real or a mere illusion? They enquired about time's properties: Can it be measured? Has it a direction or is it reversible? Does it flow or proceed from point to point? They considered time's essence by focusing on their gods Chronos and Kairos as representatives of different qualities of temporality.

The Eleatic philosophers of the sixth century BC, Heraclitus (same century) and members of the atomistic school of the fifth and fourth centuries BC developed very different and in parts opposing answers to these questions, yet we can still detect the traces of these early philosophical thoughts in contemporary theories of time in general and approaches to social time in particular.

Permanence and Change

Parmenides of Elea (sixth century BC), like his teacher Xenophanes before him, established on the basis of logic that Being was eternal and change a mere appearance. There was, both thinkers argued, no becoming, no motion, only Being extended in space. Being Is and what is cannot become, begin or cease to be. Thus it must be our senses that delude us. They are the source of the illusionary motion and change. Zeno of Elea, pupil of Parmenides, set out to provide logical proof for his teacher's theories. Through his famous paradoxes of arrows in flight, Zeno 'established' movement as illusion. He achieved this by arguing that at any one moment of observation the arrow is still, frozen in time. On the basis of logic he was thus able to 'demonstrate' that temporality (time as change) was unreal, that it was nothing but sensory delusion. Some of today's natural sciences clearly have some affinity with this notion that underlying laws constitute eternal truths, while our sense perceptions tend to create a delusory world.

An opposing perspective to the one put forward by the proponents of permanence can be gleaned from the surviving fragments of Heraclitus' theory of time. For Heraclitus (sixth century BC) everything was flux and transformation of one and the same life force. Everything derives from it and strives to return to it. To Heraclitus, therefore, the source of becoming was in the struggle between opposing forces: good and evil, hot and cold, war and peace, hunger and abundance, day and night, summer and winter. Everything requires its opposite for there to be change. Without creative conflict everything stops. Without it there is only death. In his theory we find the (Western) roots to the dialectic process. Nothing, Heraclitus suggested, is immutable in the instability of eternal flux, nothing but the law that governs it. Change is real; therefore time is real. Stability and rest are the illusion. Once more, it is the senses that deceive us. This time, however, our experience of stability is suffering from the illusion. Again, as in the work of Parmenides, truth and certainty reside in *logos* the all-encompassing world of rationality and the spirit.

Heraclitus' conceptualization of reality as flux and incessant change remained largely dormant until it was rekindled in the work of Hegel, who produced his theories in a historical context of dramatic change in all spheres of life: political, economic, scientific, technological and social.

Atoms in Motion

Anaxagoras (fifth century BC) opposed Heraclitus' theory of change with a mechanical theory of nature and substituted the idea of opposing forces with one single cause of motion. Nothing is produced from nothing. Nothing is lost. Coming into being is nothing but different mixtures of the same, infinitely small, indestructible 'germs' which are the absolute, unchangeable essence of the universe. Equally, death or passing away is nothing but the separation of a particular combination of those elements of the eternal essence. There is therefore no change, only movement, relocation, and recombination of the unit parts into different forms. The material elements are inert, without cause or purpose. *Nous*, reason/mind/spirit, is the single moving and motive force that creates order out of chaos, separates the elements and sets the cosmos in motion.

Democritus (*circa* fifth and fourth century BC), pupil of Leucippus, built on the theory of Anaxagoras and developed it in new directions. He taught that space is filled with infinite numbers of minute, indestructible particles. Democritus called these atoms, which means indivisible. Atoms, he proposed, come together, form bodies and separate again. They are in perpetual motion. Motion is part of their essence. They are not, as Anaxagoras thought, set in motion by the purpose of a transcendental principle. Instead, in perpetual motion, the atoms seek out similarity and combine according to affinities of size and form. They are caused to move and act according to necessity. In nature, Democritus insisted, nothing moves without cause, reason and necessity. There is no chance, only human ignorance. Soul, too, consists of atoms, and knowledge is inescapably dependent on the senses. Feeling is not inherent in the atoms but in their particular combinations. At death, therefore, when the combinations disintegrate, sensibility, personality and the soul cease their existence. In the atomists' theories we find the germs of classical science as it was taught until the early twentieth century, when quantum theory supplanted these fundamental ideas about atoms and the relations of parts and wholes.

Like huge waves crashing on to the seashore, the theories followed each other, each developing their philosophical argument in distinction to what had gone before: flux and eternal change, preceded by being and permanence, and succeeded by eternal motion rooted in the rearrangements of identical parts and governed by necessity and/or reason. Just as different waves are constituted from the same element, so these waves of theory shared the base assumption of a reality divided into a finite world of the senses on the one hand and an eternal realm of ideas on the other.

Eternal Noumena and Temporal Phenomena

With Plato's philosophy (*c.*429–347 BC) there is a clear reorientation from the two realms of phenomena and *noumena* towards the sphere of ideas and the ideal. The problems addressed by Plato's predecessors and his contemporaries' concerns with the motive force of motion, of permanence and change, timelessness and temporality, however, remained and had to be rethought in the light of his own dualistic theory. Like his predecessors, Plato postulated two domains. Unlike his predecessors, however, he fully theorized the atemporal realm of ideas and form. The world of phenomena, which we experience through our five senses, is the temporal realm of substance and change. Thus a tree or a plant is changing with the seasons; it grows and dies. The world of *noumena,* of the idea of the tree or plant, in contrast, is timeless. A tree's essence, its form, is unchanging. The treeness of tree, the eternal ideal of individual manifestations, is 'out of time'. It is atemporal. The idea endures, while its particular expression is perishable. According to Plato, changing phenomena are but imperfect replicas of their eternal, unchanging models. Matter is not corporeal but potential. It is the condition for creative activity. The study of nature therefore can never yield certain knowledge, only approximations. In Plato's idealist science, time does not exist in its own right but is an integral part of the universe. The universe and time are one. Marx, Weber and Durkheim, the key founders of social theory, were deeply indebted to Plato's theories and shared many of his basic premises for their very different social theory perspectives.

Form and the Measure of Motion

Aristotle (384–322 BC) was Plato's most prominent pupil. While he agreed with many of Plato's basic premises, he nevertheless placed much greater emphasis on the comprehensive study of nature and its material expression. Like Plato, Aristotle thought that we can obtain certain knowledge only from enduring form, the source of transient phenomena. For certainty, therefore, we need to penetrate beyond the ephemeral to the enduring, to the idea and form that are imposed on matter as potential. Form transforms matter into reality. Form is forming. It is goal and energy. Form as encoded future is formed dialectically through the inner contradictory essence of being. Aristotle constructed a formidable system of thought that encompassed causality, dialectics and levels of being. As such his theories are deeply implicated in the assumptions that underpin contemporary applied science.

With regard to time, Aristotle was particularly concerned with its measurement and the relation of time to motion. He came to the conclusion that time was the measure of motion, which could be expressed by number. Time and motion are mutually defining. In his *Physics* Aristotle wrote: 'Not only do we measure the movement by the time, but also the time by the movement, because they define each other. The time marks the movement, since it is its number, and the movement the time.'[2] He suggested further that we know time through the difference between before and after, which means that without change we could not know time, and without time we could not recognize change. The change he had in mind therefore was not immanent. Rather, change was the measure of difference between two states. Change and motion were transformed into the study of static states. Permanence rather than change, the timeless and the atemporal rather than transience, thus underpinned Aristotle's philosophy of nature.

And yet change in the form of decay featured in Aristotle's thoughts in an intriguing passage, which is worth quoting in full.

> Since what is 'in time' is so in the same sense as what is in number is so, a time greater than everything in time can be found . . .
>
> A thing, then, will be affected by time, just as we are accustomed to say that time wastes things away, and that all things grow old through time, and that there is oblivion owing to the lapse of time, we do not say the same of getting to know or of becoming young or fair. For time is by its nature the cause rather of decay, since it is the number of change, and change removes what is.[3]

No more is said about change except that 'it makes things depart from their former condition.'[4] From then on Aristotle's thoughts return to the measure of motion and the argument that the distance between before and after pivots around a now point which divides past and future and is ever changing. This now is tied to the body in motion just as time is tied to the number of motion.

In a last move Aristotle considers whether time could exist if there was no consciousness to measure it, 'whether, if soul did not exist time would exist or not', and he comes to the conclusion that, if only soul or reason are 'qualified to count', then without reason there could be no time 'but only that of which time is an attribute'.[5] With that final move Aristotle established that time does not belong to the temporal world but was to be located in the eternal realm of soul and reason. Aristotle's theory of time as motion was later to be adapted by Isaac Newton, while his thoughts on decay were to form one of the corner-stones of the much later scientific theories of thermodynamics and entropy. With these two elements of his time theory Aristotle straddles the thought traditions separated here into chapters 2 and 3.

Although each wave of new thoughts brought with it added levels of sophistication, the movement itself remained one between permanence, change and motion and it oscillated between an emphasis on the finite world of phenomena and the eternal realm of *noumena,* the empirical world of the senses and the metaphysical realm of ideational form. Philosophers who concentrated instead on immanent change and the relation to past, present and future are discussed in the next chapter. In this chapter I now want to take a huge leap forward to the age of science and reason because it is at this stage that time as the measure of motion makes a prominent reappearance. In the re-vision, however, the primary impetus comes not from the philosophies of predecessors but from technology. I am suggesting that a major influence on the theories of the seventeenth century was the emergence and social distribution of the mechanical clock.

Natural Science: Clockwork Universe and Change

When Isaac Newton (1642–1727) published his *Philosophiae naturalis principia mathematica,* or *The Principia,* in 1687, the clock had permeated the life of science and trade and had begun to structure social life more generally. 'The image of the clockwork extends', writes Thompson, 'until, with Newton, it has engrossed the universe.'[6] Its pervasiveness and dominant role in social transformation had rekindled interest in objective time and the measure of motion, an interest that had waned since its heyday in the philosophies of Greek antiquity, outlined above. I discuss the influence of clock time and associated social relations in chapters 5 and 6. First, however, I still need to trace the thoughts of Newton, Kant and Hegel before I focus on the role of time in the social theories of Marx, Weber and Durkheim.

As I show in other work,[7] the influence of Newton's *Principia* cannot be overestimated. It towered over the intellectual landscape of its period. Not only fellow scientists but also philosophers were compelled to engage with its theories. Newton's writings on time thus form the backcloth against which the philosophical theories of Kant, Hegel and Bergson, for example, were developed. Like Aristotle, Newton was not concerned with time in its own right but with the operational value of time as measure of motion. He conceived of time as a quantity: invariant, infinitely divisible into space-like units, measurable in length and expressible as number. Newtonian time is time taken, the duration between events, which is unaffected by the transformation it describes. This physical measure, in turn, is located in absolute time. Newton believed all things and events to have a distinct position in space and to occur at unique moments in time. He wrote: 'Absolute, true and mathematical time, of itself, and from its own nature, flows equably without relation to anything eternal, and by another name is called duration. . . . All motions may be accelerated or retarded, but the flowing of absolute time is not liable to change.'[8]

This means that Newton's physics dealt with measurements and laws which pertain to the motion of things only *in* time, on the one hand, and absolute time within which motion and change are thought to take place, on the other. Again like Aristotle before him, Newton did not deal with change explicitly as an external quantity, but incorporated time only implicitly in the description of events. His laws of motion calculated not change but rates of change. Absolute time, which he thought to be flowing continually and equally without relation to anything, had in fact been removed from the description. Newton's motion, like that of Anaxagoras and Democritus, pertained to change in position only. By eliminating all boundary conditions Newton was able to conceive of motion as reversible, as symmetrical with respect to the past and the future. His time *t* symbolized a unit length without direction. It applied to all aspects of time equally. As

Denbigh explains, Newtonian physics has no means of identifying the unique present.

> The t-coordinate is an undifferentiated continuum, and, if this coordinate is 'taken for real' as has been the tendency among many scientists and philosophers, the familiar distinction between past, present and future, so important in human affairs, comes to be regarded as a mere peculiarity of consciousness. It is as if every event along the coordinate is, in some sense, 'equally real', even those events which (to us) 'have not yet happened'.[9]

In Newton's equations, we can therefore say, motion proceeded in non-temporal time. Not only has time been spatialized but motion has been stabilized. Moreover, like the philosophies of ancient Greece, Newton's theory of time contained irreconcilable dualisms. It left unresolved the connection between absolute and measured time on the one hand and the objective time of the clock and the subjective time of experience on the other.

The Times of Change and Order

A very different picture emerges some two hundred years later with thermodynamic physics, when we can see the ancient debate between permanence and change entering the realm of theoretical physics. Thermodynamics, which originated with the work of Ludwig Eduard Bolzmann (1844–1906) at the end of the nineteenth century, is based on the realization that all forms of energy, from mechanical to thermal, are convertible to each other. This led to an understanding that was fundamentally different from the idealized world of a clockwork universe of objects in motion. It involved both a shift from time symmetry to a distinction between past and future, and a move from idealizations to descriptions of nature.

All dynamic theories conceptualize energy as being conserved. In thermodynamics, unlike Newtonian dynamics, however, energy is conserved but it cannot be reversed. Energy exchange is a unidirectional, irreversible process. This knowledge allows an observer to distinguish processes on a before and after basis. The issue of conservation, as we have seen above, has its roots in the philosophies of the atomists of ancient Greece.

Two famous laws have been formulated that make explicit the distinction between thermodynamics and Newtonian dynamics. The first law of thermodynamics deals with the conservation of energy. It states that the total amount of energy in a process is conserved despite complex forms and changes. In other words, energy can never be created or destroyed; it can only be transformed from one form into another. The second law places an important restriction on this idea of endless transformations. We know from our daily experiences that the energy that has been used to cook food, run a marathon, or drive a car cannot be used again for the same job because it has been dissipated into the environment as waste energy. This knowledge is contained in the second law of thermodynamics, which states that, while total energy is constant, *useful* energy is diminishing. It is rendered unavailable due to dissipation. We also know from experience that the reversal of those processes is impossible: we cannot 'un-run' a marathon. The environmental pollution from travelling by car cannot be reconstituted into petrol and used for another journey. The cake cannot be disassembled into its uncooked ingredients. The second law therefore expresses explicitly what is known tacitly in everyday life: that all interacting things and systems are impermanent and have an irreversible direction. Asymmetry abounds. Abstract Newtonian motion turns to interactive transformation and physical time becomes directional and irreversible.

To appreciate the changes in thermodynamic understanding that took place during the latter part of the twentieth century we have to turn to the work of the Nobel laureate Ilya Prigogine. His 'theory of dissipative structures' helps us to see better the depth of difference between the atemporal time of Newtonian science and the temporal time of what he calls the new 'science of becoming'.[10]

Prigogine developed his theory in order to explain natural phenomena and flow structures that function far from equilibrium. Prigogine's dissipative structures cover both living and non-living flowing structures such as water, sand, wind or lava, for example. Contrary to machines, which are designed to operate as close as possible to equilibrium, that is, with a minimum of energy exchange, dissipative structures are open to a continuous flow of matter and energy. A machine 'runs efficiently' if it uses and loses as little energy as possible. Far-from-equilibrium systems, in contrast, increase their stability and with it their efficiency with the degree of openness and energy exchange. That is to say, they thrive on high degrees of energy exchange because the discarded energy of one system functions as an energy source for another. In living systems this is what we understand as the ecological exchange principle.

Newton's linear, time-reversible world is a world without surprises, a machine reality that could be taken to bits and then rebuilt again. In contrast to this, the world of dissipative structures is unpredictable, non-linear, flowing, irreversible connectedness, a world of broken symmetry and timefullness. While the heat transfer in Newtonian systems of exchange produces pollution and waste, the energy transfer in dissipative structures becomes a source of order, creativity and growth.

With the shift from abstract motion to interaction, time becomes internal to the event, a system-specific process that leaves a record such as geological strata, volcanic landscapes, or river gorges. In distinction to the Newtonian *t*-coordinate, Prigogine proposed a new conceptualization of physical time. He introduced a time operator T to describe the broken symmetries of real events. This T-time is to be understood as the internal age of a system, which expresses irreversibility, directionality and an essential difference between past and future. This places Prigogine's work very close indeed to the theorists discussed in the next chapter.

Enlightenment Theories: *A Priori* and Dialectic

With the philosophies of the Enlightenment came a shift in emphasis from ontology to epistemology and a move towards questions about the source(s) of our ideas and knowledge about time. The focus changed from questions about what time is to ones of knowledge about time: is time to be sought

in external phenomena or human existence, in conceptualizations or *a priori* intuitions, in consciousness or reflexivity,
experience or language, culture or Being? The range of
choices from dualistic modes of explanation was equally
bewildering: analytic or synthetic, nominalist or realist,
logical or empirical, idealist or materialist, rational or experimental, ideographic or nomothetic.

The fact that we can explore time physically, experientially,
existentially, experimentally and through human artefacts
was given as further evidence for the hypothesis that time is
fundamentally dependent on mind, that change in nature
needs to be transformed symbolically before the idea of time
becomes possible. Despite the shift from Being to knowledge,
however, the underlying dualisms of phenomena and
noumena remained unchallenged.

In the *Critique of Pure Reason*, Immanuel Kant
(1724–1804) concluded that order was imposed on nature
by the human mind/spirit through a system of categories on
the one hand and the *a priori* intuitions of space and time on
the other. Far from being the mere measure of motion, time
in Kant's theory precedes experience and perception. It is the
conceptual tool that makes experience and perception possible. It is the 'immortal discovery of Kant', as Alfred Weber
put it, that '*space and time are original intuitions of reason,
prior to all experience*' (his emphasis).[11] Kant offered a
number of proofs to substantiate his conclusion. For children
to make sense of their perceptions, he argued, they needed to
have a temporal frame that ordered perceived phenomena
and events into a conceptual schema of before and after. Secondly, we can abstract characteristics of phenomena such as
their colour, height, lengths and smell, for example, but we
cannot abstract phenomena from time. Time is the
inescapable and irreducible remainder. A third proof is provided by mathematics: geometry as the science of space and
arithmetic as the science of duration and succession are both
independent of experience. Their truths arise from reason
alone. Finally, we cannot see time. Time does not correspond
with objects, feelings or images that appear in and over time.
It is neither an object of perception nor the result of comparative perception. Rather, time is an inherent, thus *a priori*,
mode of perception. It is of relevance therefore not to *what*

how we perceive, feel or imagine. Since time and space
inescapable modes of perception, Kant conceived of them
a seemingly paradoxical way as both empirically real and
nscendentally ideal,[12] as well as collectively formed and
ividually applied.

Kant's conclusions about the conceptual status of time and
ice have far-reaching philosophical consequences. They
an, given that all judgements are grounded exclusively in
rception and in objects of possible experience, that there is
basis for a rational metaphysics, no way of knowing the
noumenon, the thing in itself, beyond the way it appears to
us as *phenomenon*. Such a conclusion had, of course, been
reached once before in the theories of Plato, formulated in
the third century BC.

In the work of Georg Wilhelm Friedrich Hegel
(1770–1831) a number of dualisms are resolved dialectically.
Mind and matter, Being and becoming, nature and society,
the world of phenomena and *noumena*, ontology and epistemology are brought together in a dynamic whole. Time is the
condition not of perception but of consciousness. Time is. It
precedes consciousness. 'Time appears as destiny and necessity of spirit.'[13] All rational comprehension, Hegel argued,
requires underlying *logos*, a spiritual presence that gives life
to matter. Matter therefore is embodied spirit. Conversely, the
spirit requires materiality in order to be embodied. Being is
Becoming. Pure matter is meaningless since there is an
end-directedness, a 'for-ness' in all matter. Thus we can
understand the living world only with reference to the interdependence and intercommitment of its parts/members, of
which the highest expression is interpersonal commitment in
human societies. Without society there can be no spirit.
Without spirit there can be no self-consciousness. Physics
therefore cannot provide us with the meaning of time.
Instead, time can only be grasped on the basis of a historical
perspective. Process and development are conceived in dialectical terms where a totality of forces, opposing but internally
related, constitutes the motive force of history in unbroken
waves of thesis, antithesis and synthesis.

For the synthesis Hegel uses the word *Aufhebung* which,
in the German language, has a triple meaning: ceasing/
stopping/getting rid of; safe-keeping out of sight; and lifting to

a higher level. Hegel's dialectic operates not purely at the level of logic; rather, it is also applied at the level of ontology and metaphysics. The dynamic of reality is synthesized through the spirit. In Hegel as in Heraclitus, everything changes, including time. 'Everything does not appear and pass in time; time itself is this becoming, arising and passing away'.[14] He pointed out that the everyday understanding of time was predicated on an abstraction and that we need to get beyond this and understand that 'things are in time because they are finite; they do not pass away because they are in time, but are themselves that which is temporal . . . It is therefore the process of actual things which constitutes time.'[15]

With this move time is retemporalized. For the first time since the philosophy of Heraclitus, time was theorized as immanent, as internal to and constitutive of living and social systems. However, Hegel also agreed with Plato and Kant that the *notion* of time was eternal. Only that which is finite is subject to time. Ideas and the spirit are eternal.[16]

It is important to acknowledge that Hegel's thoughts on time straddle the thought traditions that are separated here into two chapters. Since, however, his work has had such a major influence on Karl Marx's theory, I have decided to locate Hegel in this chapter. It is further necessary to appreciate that Hegel's approach to time is neither prominent in his writings nor easily identified with any one of his writings. Rather, it is dispersed throughout his work. It thus needed to be gathered from across his philosophical system and is consequently open to a range of interpretations.[17] I selected above a small number of aspects from the *Phenomenology of Mind* and the *Philosophy of Nature* that show both the links to earlier thought and demonstrate Hegel's influence on the social theories of time.

Social Theory: Practice, Value and Category

With Marx, Weber and Durkheim, the founders of social theory, the direction of time focus switched once more. These theorists turned their backs on ontology and epistemology and attended instead to matters of social practice. They were concerned to move from abstract thought to social production and the creation of institutional practices and traditions. Not as Being or becoming, but as social relation, resource and value does time become an appropriate object of social science investigation. Despite the novel focus, however, the thought structures of the ancient world solidly underpinned the theories of Marx, Weber and Durkheim and as such delimited their conceptualizations in ways that are unique to each of their respective social theory systems.

The Capitalist Time Economy: Commodification and Compression

Karl Marx (1818–1883) never focused on time *per se*. He did not produce a theory of time. Despite this, however, time and temporality played a central role in Marx's conceptualization of change and historical development, on the one hand, and his economic theories of surplus value and commodification, on the other. Deeply influenced by Hegel's philosophy, Marx's dialectic was both rooted in and transcended the Hegelian version. It can be seen as the *Aufhebung* of Hegel's philosophy: it does away with it, keeps it safe and takes it to a higher plane of synthesis. Marx was concerned to purge Hegel's dialectic of its metaphysical qualities. He wanted his own dialectic to be grounded and embodied. His philosophy was to enable and empower, while his theory was to provide the knowledge base for action and deliberative change.

Where Plato and Hegel had distinguished between the temporal realms of finite being and eternity as the spirit/mind sphere of categories and logic, Marx understood the categories themselves as historically formed and forming, as products and producers of sociality. Categories for Marx were indistinguishable from their manifestations in things, events and practices. In a dialectic where thought and the material world are unified by labour into a coherent whole, both are subject to constant change. Any sociopolitical struggle had to be conceived in terms of this ongoing flux and, Marx insisted, there was a need to understand the motive force and mechanisms of that ceaseless process in order to identify the sought-after potential access points for change.

It is in a historically distinct way that we need to appreciate Marx's use of time in *Capital, Volume I* and *Grundrisse*, where it is discussed in relation to shift-work, the length of the working day, compression, commodification and exchange value. Without ever being explicitly theorized, the control, regulation and exploitation of labour time are pivotal to Marx's labour theory of value. For workers to be paid for their time rather than the goods and services they provide, time had first to become an abstract exchange value which needed to be differentiated from the use value of such goods and services. All the endlessly different products of work have use values that are always context and situation specific, as is clearly the case with, for example, the use value of a table, a coat, an operation and a pension plan. However, when we want to exchange something for money, a third value has to be introduced to mediate between the two. Unlike the use value, which is context and situation specific, this mediating exchange value has to be context independent. The common, decontextualized value by which products, tasks and services can be evaluated and exchanged is time. As Marx put it:

> Every commodity (product or instrument of production) is = to the objectification of a given amount of labour time. Their value, the relation in which they are exchanged against other commodities, or other commodities against them, is = to the quantity of labour time realised in them.[18]

Time is the decontextualized, asituational abstract exchange value that allows work to be translated into money. Since, however, money is a quantitative medium, the time that features in this exchange has to be of a quantitative kind as well: not the variable time of seasons, ageing, growth and decay, joy and pain, but the invariable, abstract time of the clock where one hour is the same irrespective of context and emotion. Only the quantitative, divisible time of the clock is translatable into money. Only this decontextualized time can serve as an abstract exchange value and thus be traded as a commodity on the labour market. Only in this decontextualized form, Marx suggested, can time become commodified on the one hand and an integral component of production on the other. In Marx's analysis, therefore, clock time is the very expression of commodified time.[19] That is to say, the use of time as an abstract exchange value is possible only on the basis of 'empty time', a time separated from content and context, disembodied from events. Only as an abstract, standardized unit can time become a medium for exchange and a neutral value in the calculation of efficiency and profit.

When time is money, then the production of something of equal quality in a shorter time allows for a reduction in the price of the product, which increases its competitiveness. Equally, the faster an invention comes to market the better for the competitive edge over business rivals. To be first, that is faster than competitors, is crucial, and this applies whether the 'product' is a new invention, garment, news story or a new drug. Thus, when time is money, speed becomes an absolute and unassailable imperative for business. At the same time, when speed is equated with efficiency, then time compression and intensification of processes seem inevitable. This argument was presented by Marx in *Capital, Volume I*[20] where he argued that in a context of competition, commodified labour time as abstract exchange value had to be intensified in order for employers to stay competitive and profitable. Competition, Marx proposed, will compel employers to intensify the energy expended by workers.

> It imposes on the worker an increased expenditure of labour within time which remains constant, a heightened tension of labour-power, a closer filling-up of the pores of the working day, i.e. a condensation of labour, to a degree which can only be attained within the limits of the shortened working day. This compression of the greater mass of labour into a given period now counts for what it really is, namely an increase in the quantity of labour. In addition, to the measure of its 'extensive magnitude', labour-time now acquires a measure of its intensity, or degree of density. The denser hour of the 10-hour working day contains more labour, i.e. expended labour power, than the more porous hour of the 12-hour working day.[21]

The means by which this intensification is to be achieved are manifold and can involve managerial strategies focused on the use of machinery on the one hand and the rationalization, mechanization and reorganization of labour on the other. All in turn are underpinned by a purely quantitative approach to time.

Marx pointed out that governments have the power to limit working hours but they have no jurisdiction over the intensity of work that is extracted from labour. Thus, as soon as laws are in place to restrict and/or reduce working hours, capital tends to compensate for this with compression, 'systematically raising the intensity of labour, and converting every improvement in machinery into a more perfect means for soaking up labour power'.[22] Commodification, compression and intensification were therefore to be sought in the quantification, decontextualization, rationalization and commodification of time, in the calculation of time in relation to money, efficiency, competition and profit.

If we now look at Marx's approach to time from a philosophical perspective we can see how Heraclitus, Aristotle and Hegel were major influences on his perspective on change and how time was immanent in the systems under his investigation. In his early philosophical writings Marx was concerned with species-being, that is, what makes the life of the human species distinct from that of animal species, and he understood nature and society as a continuum, each sphere being bounded by different socialities. Marx's time is grounded in the material conditions of historically constituted modes and relations of production. Clock time, the imposed time to human design, is internalized in socioeconomic relations and as such is a driving force of change in a particular direction: decontextualized and historical time are entwined in a dialectical dynamic.

While Marx did not consistently theorize the temporal relations of all the social systems he explored, his work on time in capitalist society suggests that time is embedded in the various technologies and economic relations and as such subject to conflicts that arise at the interstices of the different temporal spheres: nature, society, home, work, production, employer, employee, economic exchange and the money economy, for example. The socioeconomic relations involved all have their own temporal logic, each not necessarily compatible with the logic of any of the others. This then raises questions about who has the power to impose which temporal structure as norm on whom, an issue we will revisit in later chapters. With regard to the past-present-future constellation of Marx's theory we can say that Marx used the focus on the past to provide projective analyses of the present. The now is the pivot on which hinges Marx's historical analysis from the standpoint of the present, on the one hand, and the trajectory of trends and potential alternative paths, on the other.

Marx's work on commodified time and the compression of time under conditions of competition has had an enormous influence on sociological and historical studies of time, work and organization in general, and the role of abstract time for changes in work practices and organizational culture more specifically. Equally, it has had a strong bearing on archaeological and anthropological research on re/productive socioenvironmental practice, as well as feminist writing on the gendered evaluation and relations of work. Marx's effect on the temporal perspective of successors is demonstrated in the chapters on time practices with reference to technology, industrialization and globalization.

From God's Gift to Economic Resource

Like Karl Marx before him, Max Weber (1864–1920) did not discuss time and temporal issues as such and, like his predecessor, he was interested in economic relations of time. In Weber's work, however, this shared focus produced very different insights and concerns. How is it, Weber asked, that something that was considered godly and outside human jurisdiction came to be seen as an economic resource and associated with efficiency and profit. In *The Protestant Ethic and the Spirit of Capitalism* Weber established an association between general processes of rationalization, the puritan attitude to work and the appreciation of time as a precious resource to be allocated and spent with diligence and frugality. Thus, in this work, Weber identified a link between capitalist principles and practices, the Protestant work ethic, and a utilitarian, economic approach to time. Weber considered Benjamin Franklin to be an ideal exponent of that new spirit of Capitalism. He cited a long passage from Franklin's

'Necessary Hints to Those that would be Rich' (1736) in which he writes:

> Remember, that time is money. He that can earn ten shillings a day by his labour, and goes abroad, or sits idle, one half of that day, though he spends but sixpence during his diversion or idleness, ought not to reckon that the only expense; he has really spent, or rather thrown away, five shillings besides.
>
> Remember, that credit is money. If a man lets his money lie in my hands after it is due, he gives me the interest, or so much as I can make of it during that time. This amounts to a considerable sum where a man has good and large credit, and makes good use of it.
>
> Remember, that money is of the prolific, generating nature. Money can beget money, and its offspring can beget more, and so on. . . .
>
> He that wastes idly a groat's worth of his time per day, one day with another, wastes the privilege of using one hundred pounds each day.
>
> He that idly loses five shillings' worth of time, loses five shillings, and might as prudently throw five shillings into the sea.
>
> He that loses five shillings, not only loses that sum, but all the advantages that might be made by turning it in dealing, which by the time that a young man becomes old, will amount to a considerable sum of money.[23]

Time here is treated as quantitative resource that is associated with work, economic exchange and a banking system tied to interest and credit. Once time is quantified and used as an exchange value it becomes an economic variable like labour, capital and machinery, a resource that has to be handled economically: we can speak of a time economy. Weber was interested in how this approach to time emerged given that time in Christian cultures was considered to belong to God and trade in time was identified with the sin of usury. Weber found part of his answer in the rigidly organized lifestyle of monks and the sixth-century monastic orders of the Benedictines, the monks of Cluny, the Cistercians and the Jesuits.[24] He suggested that the purpose of such rationalized conduct was to overcome the natural state: the strict time discipline was to free monks from their dependence on impulses and the world of nature. It trained them objectively, as workers in the service of God, and with it ensured the salvation of their souls. Gradually, he proposed, this concern for rational action and proper time-keeping spilled over into the countryside and the marketplace until, by the end of the sixteenth century, it had become a duty, an integral part of Protestant righteous conduct. Thus, in time, the active self-control in the service of God, as it was practised by the monks, became, according to Weber, the most important practical ideal of the Protestant Reformation.[25] Puritanism, like the rational asceticism of the monastic orders, sought a way of conduct that was able to suppress emotions and spontaneous impulsive enjoyment. Like the rules of St Benedict, the doctrines and guidelines for conduct of the various forms of Puritanism pursued methodical control over the whole person. This meant that with Puritanism every Christian had to be the equivalent of a monk for all of her or his life.

Yet Weber also identified some significant differences between the two asceticisms. First, the 'otherworldly asceticism' of the monastic orders was transformed into a worldly one where faith had to be proved in worldly activity. Secondly, worldly asceticism was practised not in communities but by individuals: Puritans had continuously to supervise their own state of grace. As Weber put it, 'the Puritan felt his own pulse.'[26] Thirdly, there was no confession, no easy means of starting afresh. Salvation had to be lived out in the tangibles of everyday existence. Finally, the asceticism associated with the Protestant ethic was not one of contemplation and absence of activity but one of *rationally calculable action*. Such action implied an expectation of predictable and controllable regularity within a universally applicable time, an empty time that measured the same abstract units anywhere, any time.

Assumptions of predictability and calculability became visible in the requirement for punctuality, one of the highly praised virtues of the Protestant ethic. To expect punctuality is to take as given that people can calculate, and have control over, their future actions and that they can organize their lives in accordance with the requirement of keeping appointments at mutually agreed times. It is to relate to the future instrumentally and to hold an implicit belief that the future is not merely calculable but controllable. That is to say, people had largely ceased to see themselves in the hands of fate and at the mercy of external forces outside their control. They no longer primarily understood the future as either the realm of the unknown and unknowable, or the return of the *similar*, a characteristic of living processes. Instead, valorization of punctuality presupposed a predictable future, based on the return of the *same* and a time that allowed for identification of generally applicable points in time. Universally rationalized and sectioned, decontextualized abstract time is thus a precondition for calculable actions geared towards the appropriation of a controllable and controlled future. Clock time as the material expression of this time had become naturalized to a point of being seen as time *per se*.

The other part of the answer regarding the fundamental change from religious to economic temporal relations Weber explained with reference to secularization. For the Puritans the quest for profit was a means to salvation. Only on the basis that profit was being sought not as an end in itself but for the glory of God, and on the ground that ceaseless, frugal and ascetic activity was the means to achieve grace in the eyes of God, can we make appropriate sense of Benjamin Franklin's text. Only on this basis can we understand how the Puritans' pious, religious, self-denying, ascetic action could be so inextricably linked to the pursuit of profit and the unquestioned equation of time with money. When the religious fervour faded, only the pure economic pursuit remained and the generation of profit became an end in itself. In *The Protestant Ethic and the Spirit of Capitalism* Weber thus provided an explanation for the shift from time keeping to time accounting, time trading and time rationing, and for the gradual disappearance of eternity as measure and focus of human action.

We have to understand the Protestant Reformation as not just a religious but a sociocultural movement that, during its time, generated as much intellectual comment as capitalist developments attract today. Much of Kant and Hegel's work needs to be seen as a response to this religio-cultural change. Weber's thought, in turn, was steeped in that intellectual tradition and so much so that, according to Albrow,[27] there was no need to refer to these philosophers' work in any explicit way. Their theories had become absorbed into the intellectual status quo so that colleagues and the readers more widely of Weber's work were expected to recognize immediately any of the allusions to the philosophical tradition in general and Kant's thought in particular.

Despite the strong Kantian underpinning of his thought, however, Weber did not treat time as an *a priori* intuition. Instead, time emerges from *The Protestant Ethic* as a tool for the regulation of conduct. This of course required as pre-condition an externalized, universal time, abstracted from events and emptied of all content. Only with clock time could conduct be rationalized and purged of all emotion. Only in this form could time be harnessed for the economic goal of profit creation. Only with the time created to human design could the natural condition be transcended and rational action be subject to prediction and control. Simultaneously, however, Weber showed how the Protestant approach to time entailed a fundamental change in the past-present-future con-stellation. With the gaze firmly fixed on the future, conduct was instrumental, oriented towards achieving salvation of the soul. Bereft of the Catholic belief in redemption and the expectation that sins can be undone through confession, Protestants had to come to terms with the harsh reality of a unidirectional, cumulative, irreversible time where every action counted, where every digression meant an irrevocable step on the path to damnation, every good deed was one step closer to grace.

The influence of Weber's work on the breadth of the social sciences is extensive and a number of scholars have developed the time themes that Weber opened up at the beginning of the last century. These contemporary extensions to Weber's thoughts on time are discussed in chapter 6.

Time as Social Category

Émile Durkheim (1858–1917) was the social scientist who most explicitly reacted to philosophical theories of time and in particular to Kant's theory of time as *a priori* intuition. He was part of a circle of colleagues concerned to theorize time from a thoroughly social perspective.[28] Religion was the social institution that would give them the means by which to counter the philosophical theories since, so Durkheim's argument went, 'there is no religion that is not a cosmology at the same time that it is a speculation upon divine things.'[29] Durkheim's focus on religion, however, took his work in a direction very different from that of Weber's thoughts on religious practice and time.

In *The Elementary Forms of Religious Life* (1912) Durkheim prefigured his exploration of religion with a discussion of the categories of thought that underpin understanding: 'Time, space, class, number, cause, substance, personality, etc., they correspond to the most universal property of things. They are like the solid frame which encloses thought' (p. 9). Kant, of course, had separated out time and space from the other categories and designated them *a priori* intuitions instead. Durkheim, in contrast, treated time and space as categories because, as he suggested in a footnote (p. 9), they play the same role in thought as do number and cause: they help to order our thoughts and understanding. He then proceeded to set out his argument, which went something like this: Religion is social. Religious thought (representation) is social. Religious activities such as rites and rituals have a social function. So, if time is of religious origin, then it too is social at root, which means that it cannot predate the social as *a priori* intuition. Thus he began to set out the social nature of time.

First, Durkheim argued that we cannot conceive of time without recourse to the means by which we separate out single moments, divide and measure it. Time therefore extends beyond mere personal memory.

> It is an abstract and impersonal frame which surrounds, not only our individual existence, but that of all humanity. It is like an endless chart, where all possible events can be located in relation to fixed and determined guidelines. It is not *my time* that is thus arranged; it is time in general, such as it is objectively thought of by everybody in a single civilisation. That alone is enough to give us a hint that such an arrangement ought to be collective. (p. 10)

So far, of course, there is no disagreement with Kant who had argued that time is collectively constituted but individually expressed. The first hint of Durkheim's departure from the

Kantian perspective comes with the reference to a 'single civilisation'. Since Durkheim observed across the globe great variation in representations of time, he suggested that the category of time was historically distinct, which meant that it was socially formed and forming.

> The categories of human thought are never fixed in any one definite form; they are made, unmade and remade incessantly; they change with places and times. On the other hand, the divine reason is immutable. How can this immutability give rise to this incessant variability? (p. 15)

With this question Durkheim entered the theoretical fray that had occupied Western philosophy since its early beginnings in Greek antiquity and beyond.

Durkheim dispensed with empiricists as irrationalists. Time, he argued, cannot be discovered by observation since it is independent of particular objects and subjects of observation. When we seek time through experience, Durkheim suggested, it tends to disappear (p. 14). Apriorists, in contrast, are rational since they encompass that which transcends experience. Durkheim retained the apriorists' position that knowledge combines transcendental and experiential elements that cannot be reduced to each other. The point for Durkheim, however, was to explain the source of this transcendence, to establish its genesis and morphology. To say that it is a necessary (pre)condition was to Durkeim no explanation of origin. That which is changing its form in the course of history, he argued, must have a social source, for if there was no agreement on the meaning of time, space, number and cause, for example, all communication would be impossible; there could be no social life.

> It is the very authority of society, transferring itself to a certain manner of thought, which is the indispensable condition of all common action ... it is a special sort of moral necessity which is to the intellectual life what moral obligation is to will. (p. 18)

From here Durkheim made an extremely interesting move, which has been abandoned by his functionalist followers, or alternatively reformulated into a social constructivist position. He theorized the connection between the social and natural realms. Does it mean, Durkheim asked, that we can grasp nature only through metaphors, through symbols that do not relate to that reality? His answer to this rhetorical question was that nature does not differ radically from society. Rather, it is a less complex form of the same unbroken development. Society makes the relations between things more explicit but it has 'no monopoly upon them' (p. 18).

> Society is a specific reality; it is not an empire within an empire; it is part of nature, indeed its highest representation. The social realm is a natural realm which differs from the others only by greater complexity . . .
>
> From the fact that the ideas of time, space, class, cause or personality are constructed out of social elements, it is not necessary to conclude that they are devoid of all objective value. On the contrary, their social origin rather leads to the belief that they are not without foundation in the nature of things.[30]

Durkheim concluded his preliminary observations to the exploration of religious life by proudly stating that he has managed to retain the apriorists' position on time but extended it with an explanation of its natural causes. 'It leaves the reason its specific power, but it accounts for it and does so without leaving the world of observable phenomena' (p. 19). From there he proceeded to investigate the religions of the world in order to establish their common root elements and forms.

Durkheim's social time is both historically formed and socially pregiven as a static conceptual reference system. It is collectively made and remade, but to members of communities, societies and civilizations it appears as a fixed and atemporal frame within which events and social actions are located and positioned. In Durkheim's social science reworking of Kant's philosophy of time the assumption of illusion, so prevalent in the theories of Greek antiquity, re-emerged in a modern guise. Furthermore, while Durkheim was interested in the origin and genesis of the historically formed category, his comparative method relied on snapshot comparisons of fixed states on a before-and-after or here-and-there basis. Change and with it immanent time eluded his grasp. With regard to social perspectives on time, Durkheim's influence is widely felt in perspectives ranging from functionalism and structuralism to historical sociology and the sociology of knowledge, all of which have produced rich studies of the social relations of time. Some of this research is discussed in later chapters.

Looking back over the theories encountered in this chapter we can see that the philosophers of Greek antiquity were concerned to establish the fundamental reality and distinguish between what is real and what mere appearance. Thinkers of the modern age, in contrast, were focusing first on how we know about the real and the ideal, and second on how this relates to practice, while their disagreements centred on the ancient dualisms of permanence or change, a single motive force of history or dialectics, the realms of matter or ideas, phenomena or *noumena*. Collectively, with the exception of Hegel's conceptualization, the approaches outlined in this chapter underpin and facilitate the clock-time perspective, a conceptualization of time that is premised on an externalized, objective time created to human design. The theories presented in the next chapter have fundamentally different perspectives on the subject matter.

INTERLUDE

TIME PERSPECTIVES

Time is real
Time is ideal
Time is illusion

Time is finite
Time is infinite
Time is ephemeral

Time is spirit
Time is external
Time is immanent

Time is Being
Time is becoming
Time is being/becoming

Time is memory
Time is consciousness
Time is *a priori* intuition

Time is cyclical
Time is ephemeral
Time is unchangeable

Time is measure
Time is commodity
Time is ordering principle

Time is subjective
Time is objective fact
Time is embodied materiality

3
Time Theories II

Western Philosophy: Time Within

Eternity, Creation and Spirit

With Plotinus (205–270 AD) a new phase began in the philosophy of time. Although a Neoplatonist, Plotinus' thoughts on time go well beyond that school of Greek antiquity. They encompass insights from both Persian and Indian religious thought. Plotinus refuted the identification of time with motion and the measure of motion. He replaced what had gone before him with a powerful mystical theory of time and took a first step in the direction of understanding time as relative, preparing the way for St Augustine and much later Søren Kierkegaard to formulate theories of time that attempted both a relative and a holistic understanding. Rejecting time as external frame, motion and the measure of motion, Plotinus sought the source of time with reference to eternity, in the time before time. Since time did not exist for eternal beings, he suggested, 'it is we that must create Time out of the concept and nature of derivation, which remained latent in the Divine Beings.'[1] His intriguing thoughts on time were all-encompassing, as these extracts from *The Enneads*, the collection of his writings, demonstrate:

Time at first – in reality before that 'first' was produced by the desire for succession – Time lay, though not yet as Time, in the Authentic Existence together with the Cosmos itself; the Cosmos also was merged in the Authentic and motionless within it. But there was an active principle there, one set on governing and realizing itself (= the All-Soul), and it chose to aim at something more than its present; it stirred from the rest, and the Cosmos stirred with it . . . To bring this Cosmos into being the Soul first laid aside its eternity and clothed itself with Time: this world of its fashioning it then gave over to be a servant to Time, making it at every point a thing in Time, setting all its progressions within the bournes of Time.

The Soul begot at once the Universe and Time; in that activity of the Soul this Universe sprang into being; the activity is Time, the Universe is a content of Time.

Time is in every Soul of the order of the All-Soul, present in like form in all, for all the Souls are in the one Soul.

And this is why Time can never be broken apart, any more than Eternity which, similarly, under diverse manifestations, has its Being as an integral constituent of all the eternal Existences.[2]

These few extracts provide a window on Plotinus' perspective on time, allowing us to glimpse the mysticism of his cosmology that so deeply influenced later religious and philosophical thought on the matter.

While few time theorists today would explicitly draw on or cite Plotinus, they almost invariably quote St Augustine (354–430 AD), also known as Augustine of Hippo, who, in the years between 386 and 430 AD, produced the modern equivalent of some one thousand articles and chapters. This extraordinary legacy made him one of Christianity's most prolific thinkers. His most cited text is from Book XI of *Confessions* in which St Augustine pleads with his creator to let him into the secret of time. 'My soul is on fire', he wrote, 'to know this most intricate enigma. Shut it not up, O Lord my God, good Father.'[3] Since we know time in our everyday life in a completely unproblematic way, we can get to the depth of its secrets only by asking questions that lead to further questions, and questions beyond these. Probing the depth of time's secrets, St Augustine did not come to know time or to any conclusions. Instead he raised the unquestioned, subliminal understanding to the conscious level. St Augustine's

'theory of time' is a consciousness-raising exercise that connects him to the Creator's eternal realm on the one hand and
the temporally constituted creation on the other.

Like Plotinus, St Augustine surmised that there was no
time before creation. Time was created by God (rather than
Plotinus' All-Soul) as an integral part of his creation. 'What
times should there be', he asked, 'which were not made by
Thee?'[4] As he insisted in *The City of God*, 'the world was
made, not in time, but simultaneous with time.'[5] After lengthy
deliberations on the subject of the relation between time and
creation, St Augustine came to the conclusion in *Confessions*,
Book XI, that 'time cannot be at all without creation' and
that God the Eternal Creator is 'before all periods of time'.[6]
While St Augustine successfully theorized its source and
excluded the possibility of its objective existence in motion,
however, he had to concede that the nature of time eluded
his rational grasp.[7]

Augustine of Hippo, who was a convert to Christianity,
came to appreciate time past, time present, and future time
as the essence of the human spirit, mind, consciousness or
soul, according to which translation we rely on. For to live
life as a human being, he thought, involved the interaction of
memory, perception, anticipation and desire. Without these
aspects of spirit (soul/mind/consciousness) humans would
be incapable of living their daily lives, since knowledge, experiences, goals, fears, desires and anticipations are inescapable aspects of human perception and action. From this St
Augustine concluded that past and future did not exist outside the human spirit (soul/mind). 'It can only be', he thought,
'that the mind, which regulates this process, performs three
functions; those of expectation, attention and memory. The
future which it expects, passes through the present, to which
it attends, into the past which it remembers.'[8] In the same
vein he thought that we do not measure time but that,
instead, we compare what remains fixed in memory.

St Augustine's understanding of past, present and future as
present past, present, and present future, coexisting in the
spirit/soul/consciousness/mind, has proved a fruitful source of
inspiration through the ages and has lost nothing of its
potency even today. Both George Herbert Mead and Alfred
Schutz, for example, have taken on board this understand-

ing, first formulated at the end of the fourth century AD. Mead in particular was to readdress St Augustine's question about the reality status of both past and future in the context of twentieth-century physics, philosophy, social psychology and evolutionary theory.

Equally fundamental to contemporary theory is St Augustine's counterintuitive observation that the 'flow of time' is from the future via the present to the past. When we observe the world around us it appears as a progression from past to future. Yet, from the relative position of the Self, we must admit that life involves an unbroken chain of future-oriented decisions that bring the future into the present and allow it to fade into the past. This means that the time of mind and the time of the external world move in opposite directions. In the lived present of the Self they are fused into a unified whole. This question of the directionality of time in consciousness was later to be readdressed in the phenomenological time theories of Husserl, Merleau-Ponty and Schutz.

Existence and Becoming

In the work of Søren Kierkegaard (1813–1855) time is removed from the realm of spirit/soul/consciousness/mind and firmly located in existence: not existence generally but in individual existence. In addition, Kierkegaard mistrusted all abstractions and generalizations as solutions to problems of individual existence. Problems are solved not by what one should do but with reference to particular persons, in specific contexts and circumstances. Kierkegaard understood human existence as individual and temporal: it is being-in-the-world and being-with-others in the world. Existence is dynamic. It is becoming. Kierkegaard's theory of time and temporality was firmly located in a history of thought that reached back to questions addressed in the philosophies of Greek antiquity, that is, the relation between eternity and temporality, between time as the all-embracing measure of things and temporal existence in time, between time as the framework within which events are located and the subjective location in the moving present. Where Greek philosophers could only conceive of the difference in dualistic, oppositional terms as permanence and flux, or time and eternity, Kierkegaard's philosophy united body and mind in conjunction with temporality and eternity through the Christian notion of the spirit.

Kierkegaard's thoughts on 'the instant' are illuminating here and show how this unity might be achieved. 'The instant', Kierkegaard suggested, 'is that ambiguous moment in which time and eternity touch one another, thereby positing *the temporal*.'[9] This instant, however, was not to be conceived as the point-like, abstract division that separated an empty past from an equally empty future. Rather, it was to be understood as personal and infused with spiritual meaning. It applies, as Dreyfus explains, to 'any occasion in human life when one makes a decisive choice, a commitment which gives a definite form to one's future and a retroactive meaning to one's past. In this sense it possesses a sort of eternity.'[10] In the instance of commitment the entire past is reassessed in atonement and the future refocused for redemption. The lived unification of eternity and the now are therefore achieved by spiritual existence, by the religious life in grace.

Henri Bergson (1859–1941), whose philosophy is allied to an extensive countermovement to the Enlightenment, formulated his theory of time against the backdrop of Enlightenment thinkers' almost exclusive emphasis on rationality.[11] His theory therefore was concerned with life and all that eludes the rationality principle: becoming, change and embodied development, memory, intuition and the irrational. It offered a critique of the philosophy of identity and the metaphysics of the presence. Where Kant theorized both time and space as *a priori* intuitions, Bergson was concerned with their fundamental difference. Space, he proposed, is homogeneous, a geometric field of points where each is equivalent to all others. Space is the realm of rational, natural science investigations of (dead) matter, of that which can be chopped up and reassembled without damage to the integrity of the whole. Space is. Time, in contrast, is becoming and living duration. Explaining about Bergson's differentiation of space and time, Ann Game writes:

> Linear thinking consists in putting oneself, as an observer, outside duration . . . To think of a body occupying space is to

do so from a perspective outside the body, not from a perspective of the moving body. To be *in* the body is to be in time.[12]

Time, according to Bergson, is not accessible to rationality. Rationality dissects, divides, counts and measures. Time as the realm of novelty and creation, of the unique and the irreversible, of unbroken flow is not amenable to such division. Time is indivisible. Rationality represents becoming as a series of states: fixed, immobile and finite. For Bergson, in contrast, becoming was accessible only as a *lived* reality. It needed to be lived and intuited rather than thought about and measured. As such, becoming is inaccessible to rational investigation, with its exclusive reliance on spatialized time. Scientific investigation, moreover, concentrates on repetition and sameness, unable to encompass the temporally unique. 'Thus, concentrated on what repeats, solely occupied in welding the same to the same, intellect turns away from the vision of time. It dislikes what is fluid, and solidifies everything it touches. We do not *think* real time. But we *live* it.'[13]

What Plotinus, St Augustine and Kierkegaard sought to unify through spirit/soul/mind/consciousness seems in Bergson's work to separate out through the differentiation between the qualitative temporality of the lived *durée* and the mathematically constituted *temps* of spatial time. The distinction has inspired many successors and underpins much social science work that differentiates between qualitative and quantitative time.

The Lived Present, Dasein *and Coming into Being*

Edmund Husserl (1859–1938) is the founder of phenomenology.[14] Given that all objects exist in time and are subject to temporality, phenomenology is centrally focused on time and its role in the external world of objects on the one hand, and with the internal world of experience and appropriation in the lived present on the other. Husserl's phenomenology is concerned with the epistemological enquiry into consciousness, the lived experience of object consciousness to be precise, which involves taking a detached attitude towards the objects of perception. 'It is', explains Perry, 'like the difference between *believing* in God and thinking of myself as believing in God. In the latter case the belief is not asserted, but simply noted – God becoming only the objective component of the act.'[15]

In *The Phenomenology of Internal Time Consciousness* (1905–10) Husserl rejected the idea that we experience the world around us in a succession of nows. He equally rejected the, by then, well-established operational understanding of time as measure of motion (the clock-time view in which an empty time progresses in a linear spatial manner) and the conception of time as an empty container in which events take place and objects are located. In contrast to convention, Husserl conceptualized the present as horizontality of the flowing present in which impressions and perceptions in the now are extended by retentions and protentions. He talked of the 'living present', which features both what has been and what is to be/come. Echoing the thoughts of St Augustine, but turning the fourth-century ontological enquiry into an epistemological one, Husserl suggested about the temporality of object consciousness:

> Immanent contents are what they are only in so far as during their 'actual' duration they refer ahead to something futural and back to something past . . . we have retentions of the preceding and protentions of the coming phases of precisely this content.[16]

Husserl used the example of listening to a melody to explain the process whereby protentions and retentions are accompanying the lived present in which the melody is apprehended. In contradistinction to psychologists of his time, he insisted that even a concern with short-term memory had to fundamentally include not just the past but also the future dimension. Without an extension into both directions, he argued, one could not understand speech, appreciate music or read a text. Without retention we would not know what we had been saying so far, we would lose the thread of thought. Without protention we would be incapable of finishing a sentence since the meaning must precede its being expressed in speech.

The philosophy of Martin Heidegger (1889–1976) is heavily indebted to the existentialism of Kierkegaard and the phenomenology of Husserl, but Heidegger transcended the work of both these predecessors with a system of thought that set philosophical enquiry on an entirely new path, moving it 'from things we know to things we are, from knowledge to being'.[17] Knowledgeable action rather than knowledge was Heidegger's starting point. In the work of Parmenides and Heraclitus, Heidegger found the germs of a philosophy of Being that had been negated in two thousand years of metaphysics. With *Being and Time* Heidegger began the project of philosophical reorientation that was to accompany and permeate every aspect of his life's work. With his innovative approach Heidegger left behind any pretension about philosophy as science. His philosophy is thinking towards Being. It is forever the path, never a product. Thus the enquiry, just like its subject matter, is fundamentally and irreducibly temporal.

To Heidegger *Dasein* (Being in the world) was always inclusive of the birth-death penetration and as such allowed for objectivity and for human beings to exist temporally. Humans are *zukünftig* (future-orientated/dependent) at every moment and *gewesen* (having been/become from nothingness). Birth and death enter creatively into every moment. Their *Dasein* is therefore both horizon and presencing. Horizon and presencing, as we have seen, are not only key concepts in Heidegger's work but also in the time theories of Bergson and Husserl, which became important sources of inspiration for philosophers, psychologists and social scientists alike. Heidegger suggested further that this awareness of existence as bounded entails the fear of non-existence. Death, concern, fear (Angst) and conscience are therefore fundamental aspects of *Dasein* that force action in the present. He emphasized the *Zwischen* (the between) as not only defined by its boundary permeation but also defining it.

The 'between' which relates to birth and death already lies *in the Being* of *Dasein*. On the other hand, it is by no means the case that *Dasein* 'is' actual in a point of time, and that, apart from this, it is 'surrounded' by the non-actuality of its birth and death. Understood existentially, birth is not and never is something past in the sense of something no longer present-at-hand; and death is just as far from having the kind of Being of something still outstanding, not yet present-at-hand but coming along. Factical *Dasein* exists as born; and, as born, it is already dying, in the sense of Being-towards-death. As long as *Dasein* factically exists, both the 'ends' and their 'between' *are*, and they *are* in the only way which is possible on the basis of *Dasein*'s Being as *care*. Thrownness and that Being towards death in which one either flees it or anticipates it, form a unity; and in this unity birth and death are 'connected' in a manner characteristic of *Dasein*. As care, *Dasein is* the 'between'.[18]

The temporality of *Dasein* gives meaning to birth and death while being given meaning by them. Beginning and end and that which binds them, Heidegger argued, are always mutually defining and implicated in the analysis.

Heidegger's work on time bridged birth and death, origin and destiny, thought and action, being and becoming, time and temporality, leaving us with less irreconcilable dualisms than most predecessors and successors since. In social theory much lip-service is paid to the importance of his work but we search in vain in the theories and studies of social time for the implications of his conceptualization.

Alfred North Whitehead (1861–1947), who up to the age of sixty-three worked as a professor of mathematics, developed his extensive philosophy of science, also known as process theology, late in his distinguished academic career when he moved from the United Kingdom to the United States. He saw one of the main tasks of philosophy as the critique of abstraction, of the disattention to that which is immediately at hand and of the futile attempt to explain reality with empty categories. Thus he suggested that the measure of motion and the conceptualization of time as a spatiotemporal continuum is asserted as fact where no perception of points or instants is possible.[19] Time is an inseparable part of nature. To Whitehead it is an expression of reality rather than the empty container in which events take place. In distinction to Heidegger's attention to Being, Whitehead was concerned with *coming into being* and its processual constitution. Through the temporal notion of 'actual occasion' he sought to unify subject and object, ephemerality and endurance, the static and dynamic. Such actual occasions, he suggested, have the quality of a vector, transcend their boundaries, are implicated in each other and permeate the entire system of events.

Whitehead developed the concept of 'prehension' for this being in tune with and 'feeling' certain patterns in the process of maturation. Occasions, he insisted further, are not enduring but marked by becoming and disappearance. Only in so far as they are still implicated in successor occasions do they partake in the continuity of dynamic existence. This particular understanding was also to become a central component of G. H. Mead's theory of time. In Whitehead's work, moreover, the dynamic of actual occasions was governed by logical laws and aesthetic harmony. Whitehead drew on Plato's theory of ideas when he suggested that enacted occasions are preceded by eternal objects, such as colour, shape and number, that 'exist' only as pure potential. Thus, for example, the attribute of blue precedes its realization in an event; it exists independently of its material expression. In becoming present and on its path to maturity, the actual occasion selectively draws on those eternal objects.[20] Furthermore, the creative force of the actual occasion precedes its presencing. Finally, and most importantly, all of nature experiences. Humans, animals, plants, even rocks experience and this experience is processual and temporally extended and underpins the interrelatedness of all being.

This shift in time theory from absolute, external and objective time to an experiential, relative time within has been echoed during the nineteenth and early twentieth century in the natural sciences (astronomy, biology, geology and physics), in the arts (especially literature and the fine arts) and, a little later, in the social sciences. To exemplify this fundamental shift in perspective we will briefly focus on physicists' reconceptualizations of Newtonian time in the fields of thermodynamics, relativity and quantum theory respectively, before turning our attention to two eminent social theories of relative time.

The Sciences of System-Specific Times

For non-physicists it is probably difficult to appreciate the enormity of the changes in scientific knowledge that were

developing a century ago. For over two hundred years Newtonian physics had provided a worldview that made the
world predictable, controllable and ultimately knowable, a
perspective where uncertainty was only ever for the time
being, that is, until that missing bit to the puzzle was
researched and established in scientific laws. It was a world
in which experts who understood the scientific laws were in
control, a world of optimism where anything seemed possible. As I show in previous work,[21] the post-Newtonian world,
in contrast, is a world in which the elegant symmetry and
comforting stability are displaced by asymmetry, complexity
and indeterminacy. Non-knowledge becomes a fundamental
precondition to knowledge. In each of the various branches
of this revolution in understanding the physical world, a
reconceptualization of time accompanied the formulation of
that new knowledge. To illustrate the fundamental shift in
understanding, I outline here just two of these theoretical
positions.

Time in the Theories of Relativity

In his Theories of Relativity (1905 and 1915) Albert Einstein
(1879–1955) retained Newton's operational definition of
time, and with it the assumption of reversibility and spatial-
ity, but he relativized the measure by locating it in the framework of observation. In addition, Einstein established the
speed of light as the basis of causality and boundary to everything that is physically possible.

Einstein, like the natural philosophers and physicists
before him, used time as a measure, but he no longer understood it as absolute. He established time as relative to
observers and their frames of reference. He used the concept
of *Eigenzeit* (local, proper, or system-specific time) to elabo-
rate that distinction. With Einstein's work, therefore, time
became a local, internal feature of the system of observation,
dependent on observers and their measurements. 'Relativity
tells us there is no such thing as a fixed interval of time independent of the system to which it is referred. There is no such
thing as simultaneity, there is no such thing as "now", independent of a system of reference.'[22]

Despite the fact that Einstein's Theories of Relativity deal with acceleration speeds at or near the speed of light, the underlying principle has implications for the Newtonian science conception of time as objective and absolute. Einstein's work suggests that relative, contextual time is not the preserve of a social world. Rather, it is integral to all of nature, which includes the human social world.

Einstein's theories were also influential in making explicit the close connection between time, light and causality. Time and the upper limit to the speed of light are key to understanding causality because a causal relationship can only hold between events if they are separated temporally so that a light signal, or anything slower, can pass between them. Einstein suggested that causality can be envisaged only because it takes time for signals (such as light or sound) and objects to move across space. At the macro level of the physical world every effect is assumed to have a cause and this causality is intimately tied to the sense of order with which we experience our reality. The laws of classical physics provide a rational connection between causes and their effects and the Theories of Relativity place an upper limit on phenomena that can be causally connected. Instantaneity, simultaneity, action at a distance, synchronicity, prophecy – phenomena that are discussed in later chapters – all operate at or beyond this boundary of causality. Such temporal relations beyond causality, as we shall see, pose problems for both classical knowledge and everyday practice.

Quanta and the Dance

An even more fundamental shift in perspective emanated from quantum physics during the early years of the twentieth century. Quantum physicists such as Niels Bohr (1885–1962) and Werner Heisenberg (1901–1976) wrote with incredulity about the phenomena they encountered in the quantum world beyond atoms. As I outlined in earlier work,[23] they 'found' non-local connections and acausal events; an indivisible, dynamic, patterned whole that resisted abstraction and sequencing. At this subatomic level, nature emerged as a complicated web of relations of a unified whole. The connections, it seemed, were no longer serial and local but instantaneous. In the light of these strange processes, quantum physicists had to abandon the theory of particles in motion, which was first proposed by the Greek philosophers Anaxagoras and Democritus in the fifth and fourth centuries BC respectively and operationalized since the eighteenth century by Newtonian physics.

Quanta, it seems, are fundamentally different from atoms. The word 'quantum', as the physicist Fritjof Capra explained,[24] means a unit of action which contains energy and time. This description is based on the realization that matter cannot be separated from its activities and that it exists only in the form of energy patterns marked by appearance and disappearance. Moreover the relationships between quanta are more fundamental than the single unit. This led Capra to formulate this beautiful explanation about temporality at the subatomic level: 'There is motion but there are, ultimately, no moving objects; there is activity but there are no actors; there are no dancers, there is only the dance.'[25]

In addition to understanding the most fundamental physical reality as active, interconnected wholeness, quantum physicists had to take account of their own consciousness whenever they engaged in observation or measurement of their subject matter. The very act of observation and measurement, they realized, affected what they could see. This meant that in seeking to understand the reality, they had to include themselves and their activities in the object of their study. They had to embrace their own symbol-constructing nature and implicate their theoretical framework in the analysis. Such reflexivity and relativity, they suggested, was essential for understanding and explaining anything, anybody, and any process in the universe.

Social scientists, of course, had known for a long time that their research affects what they are studying, that it changes the nature of the phenomenon under investigation. In the social sciences, however, this recognition was considered to pose an irresolvable dilemma for the scientific status of their research since 'objectivity' was still one of the most fundamental requirements of science. Since the early twentieth century, quantum physicists such as Heisenberg have established this Newtonian imperative as an impossibility and the disembodied, decontextualized scientific perspective as a fiction of the classical science imagination. If contemporary physicists can embrace temporality, relativity and reflexivity, why then is it proving so difficult to find public approval for such an approach in the social sciences, one might want to ask.

Social Theory and the Past, Present and Future

All social theorists, whether they take an objectivist or relativist position, agree that the human condition and social life cannot be understood without an inclusion of time in terms of past, present and future. Only two of the founders of social science, however, have written explicitly on this subject matter. George Herbert Mead asked ontological questions and considered the reality status of past, present and future. Alfred Schutz, in contrast, enquired about their epistemological status, their place in consciousness and their role in the construction of everyday knowledge. He was concerned to understand the past, present and future phenomenologically.

At the end of his life, George Herbert Mead (1863–1931) was working out his past thoughts in a dialogue with Whitehead's philosophy and early twentieth-century physics. *The Philosophy of the Present,* widely regarded as Mead's most important work on time, consists of lectures written shortly before his death and was published posthumously.[26] In this book Mead focused first on the emergence of the 'now' in relation to what has been in the past and then related these thoughts to his work on the nature of sociality. To explain change, continuity, the self or identity, Mead took a consistently temporal and relative standpoint, focusing exclusively on the 'time in' things, events, perspectives or roles rather than the time of an abstract framework within which experience is conceptualized. He denied reality status to the abstract time of clocks or calendars and considered it nothing more than a convention.

For Mead the present implicates past and future. Any reality that transcends the present, he argued, must exhibit itself in the present and inescapably includes becoming. If it did not, we would not be able to distinguish one event from another; we could not know time. For us to be able to conceive of the present, change and continued existence, Mead suggested further, there had to be becoming and disappearing. 'There must be at least something that happens to and in the thing which affects the nature of the thing in order that one moment may be distinguishable from another, in order that there may be time.'[27] In distinction to Parmenides's world of atemporal existence, for Mead 'the world is a world of events.'[28]

With respect to the past, Mead explained in *The Philosophy of the Present* how it was customary to think of the past as fixed, as something that cannot be changed (p. 11). Yet, in the way the past is preserved, evoked and selected, it is open to change and thus could be considered to be as hypothetical as the future. From the standpoint of the emergent present, the past is continuously recreated and reformulated into a different past. This means that the past has no status apart from its relation to the present.

> When one recalls his boyhood days he cannot get into them as he then was, without their relationship to what he has become; and if he would, that is if he could reproduce the experience as it then took place, he could not use it, for this would involve his not being in the present within which that use must take place. (p. 30)

Mead proposed further that our past is continuously reconstituted with reference to the future. A self-conscious act thus fundamentally embraces both past and future. It stretches beyond the immediate perceptual horizon and gets filled with memory and anticipatory imagination. To Mead the source of time was to be located in this process of forming pasts and futures. It meant that past and future were ideational, something representational that involves adjustment and selectivity. Through mind, we transcend the present and extend our environment. Through mind, past and future are open to us in the present. The real past, just like the real future, is unobtainable. In Mead's late work, therefore, we can discern the unbroken conceptual tradition from Whitehead and quantum physics via Husserl and Kierkegaard to St Augustine.

A number of conceptual implications arise from Mead's approach to time. First, what has taken place is implicated in what is taking place and the future potential informs what is happening in the present. Secondly, in contrast to objectivist perspectives on time, Mead understands time with reference to the becoming event. Not passage, not motion, not measurement but emergence was the source of time. Without it there could be no time, not even a quantity to be measured. Thus, according to Mead, if we think we are measuring empty intervals, we suffer a 'psychological illusion'.[29] This may sound much like Bergson's insistence on the necessary link between time and emergence, but Mead, in distinction to Bergson, does not imprison temporal time in the intro-spective realm but understands it as interactively and inter-subjectively constituted.[30] Mead's approach, moreover, allows for no overarching universal time standard because all that we know must be done from the perspective of the organism that does the knowing, measuring or dating (note the link here to the Theories of Relativity). Clock and calendar time may be objective, Mead conceded, but this ex-ternally constituted time is never independent from the perspective of the knower. The fact that time is abstracted worldwide in this particular way makes this time abstraction no less an attitude of each user.

From this brief account we can see how Mead has con-structed a conceptual web that has the potential to radically alter the way social time is understood and theorized.

Matters Concerning Epistemology

Of similar importance to social science is the time theory of Alfred Schutz (1899–1959). The phenomenologist Schutz sought to understand the everyday experience of ordinary people and in the process he inevitably encountered time and temporality as an integral aspect of social interaction and the construction of meaning. In agreement with Weber, Schutz's starting point was action and, following Husserl, his specific focus was the experience and constitution of intersubjective, intentional consciousness. Clearly, space, time and temporal-ity are universal features of both the experience and the constitution of everyday life. Issues of past, present and future consequently feature prominently in Schutz's theory. They enter into his work on action, meaning, communication, social relations of the personal and impersonal kind, the taken for granted realm of practical activity and the effortless negotiation of multiple lifeworlds.

In *The Problem of Social Reality* Schutz focused on different temporalities of the 'act' and 'action' respectively. An act, he suggested, can only be known retrospectively, once it has been performed. As rationalized act it is explained with reference to the past. It can also be projected into the future as a potential act. Knowledge about any act as an act – past or future – therefore requires reflection. In contrast to the act, action is intimately tied to the present. It is a process with a forward direction, orientated towards projects. Action is always projected action and lived in an ongoing process. Action, therefore, is always present, lived action in the direction of the future, while the act is always rationalized from a present (even the projected future present) in the direction of the past. This means meaning is inescapably attributed reflectively.

Extending Mead's argument, Schutz suggested that we could be aware of our stream of consciousness only in the reflective mode, which entails on the one hand a 'stepping outside' the stream of consciousness and future orientated action, and on the other a looking back at previously performed or imagined acts.

> We cannot approach the realm of the Self without an act of reflective turning. But what we grasp by the *reflective* act is never the present of our stream of thought and also not its specious present; it is always its past. Just now the grasped experience pertained to my present, but in grasping it I know it is not present any more. And, even if it continues, I am aware only by an afterthought that my reflective turning towards its starting phases has been simultaneous with its continuation. The whole present, therefore, and also the vivid present of our Self, is inaccessible for the reflective attitude. We can only turn to the stream of our thought as if it had stopped with the last grasped experience. In other words, self-consciousness can only be experienced *modo praeterito*, in the past tense.[31]

The stream of consciousness, Schutz seems to be arguing, is always in the action mode even while it is engaged in reflecting on past or imagined acts. Actions may be grasped intuitively as a totality in the 'vivid flowing present', but acts, which have their meaning attributed reflectively, have a different temporal structure within the stream of consciousness. Since reflection and re-presentation break the flowing unity, the quality of the whole cannot be retained once it has been subject to rationalization.

Moreover, aspects of past acts need to be selected from the vastness of the totality of past and potential acts. We select, Schutz argued, from within a horizon of social relatedness and establish causal relationships and rationalizations. In addition to selection we both order according to priorities and sequence with reference to a hierarchy of values and necessities. Selecting, prioritizing and sequencing, therefore, form part of the taken-for-granted strategies that people employ in their routine interplay of act and action. These temporal strategies in turn are bounded by the socially constituted common stock of knowledge, by language and the collective systems of relevance.

These common aspects, Schutz noted, are historical in nature, sedimented over long periods of community life and embedded in the common-sense world in which people operate as physical and social beings with unique biographies. People orient in this common-sense world, he suggested further, from a personal temporal perspective where their actual here and now is the central point of reference from which all other orientations follow. This means that people are grounded in subjective time while simultaneously being rooted in the intersubjective reality of common sense.

In Schutz's work on time, therefore, the focus is on the difference between doing and rationalizing what has been done. Those differences in turn are closely tied to language as fundamentally tensed and to the ability to conceive of pasts and futures in a multiple way. From this temporal perspective we can think of future futures, future presents, present futures, future pasts or any number of other combinations. As in Mead's work, in Schutz's time theory the present as the locus of action and communication is accorded special status.

For all theorists discussed in this chapter past, present and future were of central importance to (social) life. All accorded the present a privileged position but diverged in their conceptualizations of it. While for St Augustine past and future coexisted in a present, for Mead past and future have been not only implied but also represented, projected, recreated and constructed with reference to a present. The phenomenologists Husserl and Schutz acknowledged that we act and communicate in the present but cautioned that this was not possible without protentions, retentions and the past–future penetration since reflection, sedimented knowledge, projects and anxieties are inextricably bound to everyday life interactions. In Heidegger's work the past and future of Being came to be identified with birth and death, while *Dasein* pointed to a present permeated by this beginning and end of individual existence.

In this chapter we have seen how focus on past, present and future confronts us with the contextual, constructive, experiential and relative world of processes where past and future change with each new present and each present is defined with reference to a particular event, system, biography or person. And yet, in everyday life, the relative temporality of past, present and future and the objective time of calendars and clocks are not chosen on an either–or basis. Rather, they coexist, interpenetrate and mutually implicate each other. We move between those temporal worlds with great agility, giving little thought to the matter and are unperturbed by their conceptual and logical incompatibility. We construct them from the position of the present and accomplish their smooth integration in daily social practice. It is time as practice that we turn to in the next part of this book.

In the chapters that follow, the emphasis shifts from theory to practice. The chapter on time practices of cultural transcendence reconnects to the time stories and provides a bridge to temporal conditions and practices associated with the industrial way of life. We therefore become involved in explorations of both what is shared by humanity and what is historically and culturally unique. Understanding of these unique and shared temporalities becomes particularly pertinent at a point in history when the globalization and unification of time through the creation of world time, standard time and time zones is highlighting more intensely than ever before the global diversity of temporal relations and related inequities in power, opportunity and life chances.

Not all aspects of time and temporality detailed in part I of this book have survived equally well through the ages. In a world structured around a time created to human design, it seems, the inescapable spectre of human contingence recedes into the background of existential concern. With the taken-for-granted dominance of clock time the question of transcendence seems to lose some of its pertinence and the threat of time its central role in social thought and reflections on the human condition. In such a socioeconomic context, understanding can be achieved only by considering the social relations of time, that is, people's involvement with time through particular practices and technologies. This requires that we give attention to time as theory in practice, experience in explanation, lived orientation in material expression.

Part II
What is the Role of Time in Social Life?

We cannot understand time as a key concept through stories and theories alone. Rather, we need to look at practices and temporal relations, that is, at our involvement with the world. As the archaeologist Christopher Gosden notes, 'People create time and space through their actions. Time and space, in turn, become part of the structure of habitual action, shaping the nature of reference between actions.'[1] When we look at cultural practices we see myths, philosophies and theories enacted. Each of the chapters in this second part of the book engages with different aspects of temporal practice and engagement with nature's processes. Chapter 4 focuses on cultural means to transcend the finitude of earthly existence. It thus shows Heidegger's theory of *Dasein* in action. Chapter 5 is concerned with knowledge for action, derived from theories relating to the planetary cycles of eternal return. Chapter 6, finally, details some of industrial societies' strategies and efforts to own time and gain control over that which appears to be distinctly beyond control.

Cultural practice creates social time and, conversely, in their relationship to time human beings create culture and structure their social lives. This duality is the focus of part II of the book where we shift emphasis from stories and theories about time, to theory-impregnated time practices and their cultural effects. Underpinning the chapters on knowledge practices is the suggestion that the relationship to finitude is ineradicably implicated in cultural practice and that the variable responses to this primary threat are not only tied up with cultural difference but also driving cultural change. This position is developed against the background of a vast body of work on the relationship to finitude that comprises a wide range of disciplines from cultural history and theology to depth psychology and philosophy. Thus, for example, the psychologist Ernest Becker, in his seminal *The Denial of Death*, proposed that 'the idea of death, the fear of it, haunts the human animal like nothing else; it is the mainspring of human activity.'[2] Similarly, Heidegger suggested that the fear of non-existence forces action in the present.[3] In response to this existential condition, it seems, people create cultural means of achieving immortality: heroism and fame that outlast individual existence, religions that promise a life after death, a spirit world that transcends us. We speculate about origins and infinity. We maintain myths and rituals that connect us to origins and destinies and locate us in the wider scheme of things. We establish institutions that outlive their individual members and thus allow us to forget that our practices are delimited by personal beginnings and ends.

Whether death means terror or is accepted in quiet resignation, it seems difficult to accept the end of life as the end of being. The earliest myths told stories that responded to this inescapable source of insecurity. All the great religions provided beliefs that pandered to this most existential of concerns. It is, I think, safe to say that in no known society are members left to face death uninitiated. Rather, it is a mark of human culture that persons are provided with beliefs and rituals that ensure proper passage to a realm beyond death. This applies whether the life after death is to be in the ancestral netherworld, the Christian heaven and hell, or tied to a journey of reincarnation. As far as it is possible to tell from archaeological and historical records, humans have constructed their being eternally and surrounded themselves with symbols of permanence. I therefore want to argue that the development of human culture, that is, the form of life and practices embodied in traditions, institutions and artefacts, is inextricably tied to the relationship to time. It is bound to approaches to finitude, transience and decay, and to the human quest for transcendence of the earthly condition.

How cultures and their members relate to time has changed through the ages and with specific contexts. Accordingly, the industrial way of life has its own unique time practices, which are the subject matter of chapters 5 and 6. 'In Pursuit of Time Know-how' is concerned with measurement and the application of technologies to impose a cultural stamp on temporality. Despite their diversity, all industrial time practices depend on time first being created to human design, that is, as abstract, decontextualized and quantifiable clock time. Built on the foundations of clock time a time economy could flourish and the connection between time and money be established. Time could become commodified, compressed and controlled. These economic time practices could then be globalized and imposed as norm the world over. The last chapter on 'The Quest for Time Control' is thus focused on both the practices and some of their socio-environmental effects. Again, these chapters are not intended to be comprehensive. Like the chapters in part I, they seek to open a window on the subject, provide first sightings of the complex and fascinating terrain, identify some of the important work in the field and open up the topic for further inquiry.

INTERLUDE

TIME TRANSCENDENCE

Cycles
Faced with cycles we create lines
Faced with spirals we produce circles
Faced with cycles of return we seek nirvana
Faced with rhythmic cycles we devise the clock

Change
Faced with change we create stability
Faced with variation we produce sameness
Faced with uncertainty we establish the sciences
Faced with directional change we fashion reversibility

Transience
Faced with transience we hold time still
Faced with ephemerality we impose structure
Faced with impermanence we create permanence
Faced with mutability we produce art and institutions

Decay
Faced with decay we invent preservation
Faced with decline we attempt to reverse it
Faced with entropy we produce ever more of it
Faced with deterioration science creates irradiation

Mortality
Faced with death we crave an afterlife
Faced with mortality we seek immortality
Faced with extinction we presume reincarnation
Faced with finitude we produce things that outlast us

4
Cultural Practices of Time Transcendence

In this chapter we are concerned with practices and temporal relations that are shared by cultures through the ages. Accordingly, we draw primarily on the writings of anthropologists, archaeologists and historians. While the detail and form of particular time transcendent practices may be expressed differently at different historical periods, the principles that underpin them are common to humanity. Thus, as Gosden insists with reference to the socio-natural relations of time, 'There has never been a period in the last 3.5 million years in which natural rhythms were human rhythms, and we have no evidence that Palaeolithic groups were in tune with, or at the mercy of the environment.'[1] And yet, despite the strong evidence to the contrary, classical descriptions from anthropology, theology and history tend to make sharp distinctions between archaic and modern societies.[2] Temporal relations and practices play a key role in the definition of those distinctions. Archaic societies were said to have lived in cyclical time, in a time of eternal return. They were embedded in nature, it was argued, and governed by nature's rhythms. Modern societies, in contrast, were said to operate in linear time with substantial past and future extensions. In contrast to archaic societies, it was suggested, modern societies have extricated themselves from the cycles of nature and live according to sociocultural rhythms. While temporal horizons of ancient societies were delimited by the seasons, so the argument went, ours are historical, extending to the distant past and especially the long-term future.[3]

While there is no doubt that the temporal relations of archaic societies are different from those of 'modern' societies, we will see that they are no less complex, sophisticated or temporally extended. On the contrary, the cultural reach into past and future, and with it the transcendence of individual lifetimes, appears to have been far greater in archaic societies than is the case for contemporary industrial societies, for example. As members of the 'modern' world few of us could say that they are in frequent communion with the spirit world that awaits us at the end of our earthly journey. Few of us could claim to be conscious bearers of thousands of years of tradition. Archaic cultures could. And where their stories of temporal relations and records of their activities have survived, these give us a window on some of the time practices that structured archaic life, both sacred and profane.

It is through the effort to make time stand still, to create permanence in the sea of change and to engage with mortality, that most of what we today understand as culture has evolved. To quote Reanney:

> From this yearning for forever, this aching sense of passing time, springs most of humanity's greatest achievements in art, music, literature and science. Paradoxically, it is the very awareness that life is fleeting on the wings of time that directs human activity towards the creation of artefacts that possess the durability their creators lack, images in carved stone and marble, words written in books, beauty woven from sound, ideas captured on film. Most of civilisation is a by-product of the quest for immortality.[4]

It is the practices associated with this transcendence of time that are the focus of attention in this chapter.

Making Time Stand Still

There are numerous ways to respond to the transience, ephemerality, contingence and finitude of human existence, numerous means to impose a sociocultural will on the times of the cosmos, nature and the body. One of these is to make time stand still. The forms this takes and the meanings it carries for social groups, however, differ significantly with the particular practices employed, and the historical periods within which they are enacted.

Myth and ritual are primary means to arrest time. In their performance the original deed or decree is enacted in the present and the meaning recreated and preserved in its original form. Through the performance the enfolded past is activated and revealed, *ab origine*, that is, true to the beginning. Thus, Mircea Eliade suggests, 'myths serve as models for ceremonies that periodically reactualize the tremendous events that occurred at the beginning of time.'[5] Here practices connect to the stories recounted in the first chapter. The reassembly and embalming of Osiris's body by Isis, for example, is ritualized and re-enacted in the tomb culture of ancient Egypt. Osiris's resurrection to a life in the otherworld became the exemplary model for death as a journey to life in another realm, to be enacted whenever death has occurred. Another example could be drawn from Australian Aborigine culture where authentic existence is tied to (re-)enactment of what had been laid out for humans in those days before the beginning of time. It was during the Dreaming phase that the spirits set the world in motion and decreed appropriate conduct.

Furthermore, for archaic societies reality was actualized in repetition of 'primordial acts' and, according to Eliade, has reality status only to the extent that these have been 'posited *ab origine* by gods, heroes, or ancestors'. Eliade goes on to cite numerous texts from across the world that substantiate his point, including the Satapatha Brāmaṇa (VII, 2, 1, 4), which states that 'We must do what the gods did in the beginning', and the Taittirīya Brāmaṇa (I, 5, 9, 4), which insists: 'Thus the gods did; thus men do.'[6] Eliade goes so far as to suggest that for archaic society,

> An object or an act becomes real only insofar as it imitates or repeats an archetype. Thus, reality is acquired solely through repetition or participation; everything which lacks an exemplary model is 'meaningless', i.e. it lacks reality.[7]

When a myth is actualized in ritual, a simultaneity of existence is created. The ritual binds into one unity the originary act and the re-enactment. It brings together in the present ritual participants with the sources and forces of reality. We can speak of an active presencing of origin.[8] In this process of presencing, the time of sequence, passage and duration is negated. Time is not abolished,[9] however. Rather, it is rendered non-temporal and ahistorical. In the effort to bridge the gap between profane time and eternity the former is actively bracketed (*aufgehoben*) and the latter explicitly activated through the performance of ritual. In rituals, as in myths, original moments are reproduced, and in their repetition a reality is created where all of time becomes fulfilled in the present.[10] In a temporal context where connections are established outside profane time and space, causal relations become irrelevant while synchronicity gains in importance.

The anthropologist Claude Lévi-Strauss made a seemingly similar argument in *The Savage Mind* when he suggested that myths are machines for the suppression of time, that they resemble loops rather than a forward movement. He even defined them as reversible and non-cumulative. This, however, is a problematic conceptualization since it theorizes myths in abstraction, untold and unperformed. While we can concede that myth and ritual keep temporality at bay, their performance is inescapably temporal: it has a beginning and end, a prescribed sequence and duration; it proceeds at a specified pace and is characterized by very precise timing of the component parts. Moreover, only in their performance can myth and ritual be said to be alive, to exist. Without their being told, played, performed, read, or thought about, they have no meaning or reality. Moreover, we can never step in the same river twice, to use the Heraclitean metaphor, perform rituals backwards or untell myths. It is this dual temporality – the ritual and its performance, the timelessness of the act and the temporality of the action – that gives myths and rituals their specific character. It thus involves the presencing of origin, gathering up disparate times in a non-temporal realm beyond profane existence, together with the performance that is inescapably tied to the temporality of embodied practices.

If we think of rituals as practices of repetition that hold time still by connecting the present to origin, then it may be illuminating to briefly compare this ritualistic time practice to a contemporary repeating practice. A record or compact disc of a Beethoven piano concerto can be repeated at will in order to activate the original performance in which the musicians performing the piece sought to re-produce something that originated in earlier times. While a live performance of a Beethoven piano concerto has some similarity with the time structure of archaic myths and their ritual performance, in the majority of cases listening to a recording does not. Most listeners make no effort to connect to origin. They have no intention of gathering up Beethoven's first performance in order to fuse the two experiences. Instead, they tend to pull the music into their personal spheres. The music may take them back to earlier periods of their lives, evoke personal memories or serve to create a particular mood. Only a rare exception to the contemporary CD listener would seek to bracket the intervening time in order to make the first performance of that piano concerto part of their living present.

A second way of making time stand still relates to the externalization of knowledge through representation. To hold in unchanging form what is moving, changing and interconnected is an achievement that has been realized by our earliest ancestors through their art. It is here that we also find the first evidence of abstract representation in the form of squares, parallel lines, grids, and rows of dots. Why people painted cannot be the focus here but, regardless of whether it was used for religious, communicative and/or mythical reality-creating purposes, the effect on human time was fundamental. Art externalizes and fixes beliefs, experiences, expectancies, fears and hopes in a form that can be shared (as well as variably interpreted) by many people across generations. Once objectified, the artistic creation not only becomes a source for reflection and understanding, but also a way of passing on culture without the need for either the co-presence or even the existence of those who do the communicating. It is a way of accumulating wisdom outside the temporal, finite body and beyond the knowledge of individual persons. Written language shares with art the principal temporal relations of fixing and stabilizing what is transient and ephemeral through the externalization and disembodiment of knowledge.

We know that people use their creations as tools for understanding the world. As externalized reflections of reality, the creations, in turn, can become sources for understanding reality. Objectified, something can be grasped with the full complement of our senses, adding several dimensions to the auditory one of speech, and the auditory-visual communication between co-presents. Not only does objectification change the quality of the knowing but it also changes reality. Re-presenting and creating the temporal world in static and permanent form therefore means the reality thus created appears as if it were fixed and immutable. In this static form it facilitates reflectively based knowledge and with it a time distanciation that far exceeds that of spoken (embodied) symbolic language. Our earliest ancestors, it seems, have fashioned their creations mostly in enduring and encapsulated forms. This enabled them to reflect on the nature of their world and themselves. As such it opened new horizons of the mind and allowed for free movement in times past and future. A highly active and creative engagement with temporality and ephemerality, we can therefore surmise, is the mark of human culture.

Not only myths and art but also the earliest forms of monumental architecture can be viewed as expressions of the human endeavour to create stability and permanence, to know about the meaning of existence, about origin and destiny. All define the world from the human centre, provide a place for human beings in the scheme of nature, and provide substance, security and continuity for communal life. We can conjecture that megaliths, for example, enabled Neolithic peoples to maintain contact with that which transcended their own being, that the form of these buildings directed attention to a metaphysical source of being.[11] Megaliths unified time, space and the sacred. To the architect Keith Critchlow, the composition of megalithic temples suggests a time consciousness that embraces becoming while simultaneously unifying eternity and the now. It demonstrates a relation to the past and future of daily life, the cosmos and the sacred, and points to efforts to create harmonious concordance between heaven and earth.

The circular structure of megalithic temples is of symbolic significance because the circle is widely recognized as the most sacred representation. The full circle expresses undifferentiated space and a totality of time. Accordingly, the completed circle has to be seen as a *chosen* tactic to unify the one with the whole and to gather up, in the now, the whole of time. The time of the circle, therefore, signifies not the eternal round of seasonal activity but rather an *active creation* of eternity in the present. In this enfolding of the origin, we may surmise, lies the power of the temporally extended collective and the source of all future possibilities. Moreover, the importance of the circle extends beyond this active closing of the periphery to its centre. As Critchlow explains:

> The centre is the controlling point and represents, by a projection into the third dimension, the ontological axis and is thereby symbolically outside time and space. The centre is simultaneously the non-directional point and the non-measurable moment. Because the centre is indivisible (a-tomic) it symbolically represents the primal unity which is both source and goal of the existent.[12]

Such an interpretation of the temporal structure of megaliths and the associated social time of ancient societies has implications for social theory in general and for anthropology and archaeology in particular. Quite clearly, the cyclical, atemporal time of myths, rituals, art and sacred architecture cannot be contrasted in a meaningful way with the linear time or 'timefullness' of chronological dating and clock time, which is the taken-for-granted base on which the classical dualistic analyses were constructed. Instead, archaic practices that made time stand still need to be recognized as *creative* acts of time transcendence, as collective means to overcome the threat of non-existence, finitude and transience. They need to be appreciated therefore as cultural responses to 'the fall', the earthly condition that forms a central part of the pervasive genesis myths described at the beginning of this book and revisited in the next section of this chapter.

Knowing Fate, Forging Futures

In the myths that tell of a fall from paradise, a departure from dream time or a descent into a dark age it often was the quest for knowledge that resulted in the loss of eternal and enlightened existence. Time is the metaphor that symbolizes the descent into the (intellectual) darkness and wilderness. Past and future, mortality and finitude, transience and decay emerge as characteristics of the human condition after 'the fall'. The present becomes the locus from which knowledge of both past and future has to be constructed. The past has to be culturally reconstructed and preserved in the present through a variety of individual and collective aids. Moreover, the fallen ones encounter death but do not know their end, their fate, their future. The future is opaque, requiring their most creative skills to gain rare glimpses of what remained the exclusive preserve of their God/gods.

The quest to unlock the secrets of fate, to probe the mysteries of the future and to make contact with the not-yet-existent is shared by archaic and modern cultures. Throughout the ages, these investigative practices have taken numerous forms and many different kinds of gifted specialists have been entrusted with this important task. In his history of divination, John Cohen gives accounts of over one hundred ways of telling the future.[13] Precognition and foreknowledge were the special gifts of gods and their prophets, of oracles and seers, witches and wizards, astrologers and scientists: each one drawing on different sources for their privileged knowledge, each one using different methods to access the temporal realm beyond the senses. A few examples will serve to illustrate the way time transcendence was (and is) practised with respect to the future. This quest for knowledge of the realms beyond the present needs to be distinguished from the creation of the future, the conjecture *about* future events differentiated from cultural forays *into* the future, that is, from cultural activities that seek to control the future and in the process create successors' presents. The latter will be outlined briefly at the end of this section and revisited in the last chapter on the time politics of colonization.

The Old Testament is replete with stories about prophecies, oracles, revelations and dreams. Thus, for example, eighteen of the thirty-nine books of the Old Testament carry the subtitle 'The Book of the Prophet', telling of things that came to pass, of prophets employed to guide the Israelites on their way to freedom, of prophets as conduits to God's messages, and of the future being revealed in dreams. In Genesis (6: 13 onwards) God speaks directly to Noah, warns him of the impending flood that will destroy all of creation and instructs him to build an ark in which he is to save his family and the animals, two of every kind. In contrast to Noah, who was able to escape the flood by following God's instructions, Joseph accurately interpreted the Pharaoh's dreams and thus saved the kingdom from ruin, while Moses relayed God's commands to the Israelites. In the New Testament, too, all the significant elements of Christ's life are prophesied, as are the end of the world and Judgement Day.

Prophets of the Bible, with their privileged access to a time that is inaccessible to the senses, were depended on extensively to give guidance and forewarning, signal and council. Their foreknowledge, however, was not based on their own clairvoyance or wisdom; rather, it was imparted to them by God. What was an integral part of early Judean and Christian life, however, became in the Middle Ages a precarious gift that was likely to get you burnt at the stake. That is, any visions of the future that could not be linked unambiguously to instructions from the Divine could only be the work of Satan. Alternatively, they were blasphemous as they usurped powers that belonged to God alone. Whether the prophecies were deemed blasphemous or Devil's work, the Church's response was hard and merciless. A notable exception were the prophecies of Michel de Nôtradame – Nostradamus – a sixteenth-century physician and astrologer who managed to publish his prophecies in the form of ten individual volumes in which he foretold the future of humankind. His services as a prophet were sought by royalty and nobility well beyond the borders of his native France.[14]

In ancient Egyptian culture the relationship to the future took a different form. Here, too, foreknowledge of the future was the gift of gods. Like its biblical counterpart, ancient Egyptian society greatly depended on prophecy for guidance to conduct and forewarning of impending disaster. Unlike biblical prophets, however, Egyptian oracles and divinations were primarily connected to festivals and associated with temples. It was in this way and at these specific times and places, Jan Assmann suggests, that 'the city deities exercised their de facto rulership', which 'reached beyond the temple enclosures and included the entire citizenry'.[15]

More significant than the prophetic capacities of the gods, furthermore, was the ancient Egyptians' knowledge of the future through the anticipation of life after death and numerous detailed instructions about what to expect and how to behave to ensure a safe journey to the otherworld.[16] The instructive texts were written on the walls of tombs, on clay tablets and much later on papyrus. In ancient Egyptian society death was seen as a key marker in the stream of existence, a difficult staging post beset by perils and unforeseen hazards. By following the examples of gods, and especially Osiris, the texts rendered the unknowable accessible to ritual practice. They transformed the abyss of the great unknown into something familiar and unthreatening. Thus, for example, the 'Book of the Dead'[17] is a book of spells whose sole purpose it is to ease the journey of the dead person to the afterlife. The 'Book of what is in the Underworld', in contrast, describes the underworld, thus taking away some of the fear of the future unknown. It exists in many versions and has been found in the tombs of both kings and ordinary citizens.[18] The 'Pyramid Texts', finally, are intended to ensure entry of the dead to the afterlife. They mostly recount the Osirian legend and give detailed guidance on how to emulate Osiris's transition from the world of the living to the realm of dead souls.

Underpinning all these instructions was a belief that the preserved physical body was essential to securing existence in the afterlife. Detailed knowledge of the unknown, that is, the stages of death and the journey to the realm of the dead, provided existential security. Clear instructions for rituals relating to the deceased transformed the ministering to the dead into an essential life-giving activity. Non-existence, the ultimate unknown, had been rendered knowable. From the secure basis of practical knowledge, the future in the otherworld of dead souls became for ancient Egyptian societies a technological challenge and a matter of correct ritual conduct.

The oracles of ancient Greece obtained their privileged place in history through the famous myths that have survived through the ages and became absorbed into contemporary folklore. In almost every Greek myth, the oracle is consulted. Few decisions of significance seem to have been taken without first seeking advice from the oracle, the most famous of which was located in Delphi, the place Zeus had declared the centre of the universe.[19] The stories of Perseus and the Gorgon, of Hercules and of Oedipus, for example, all tell of attempts to avert the destiny prophesied by the oracle. In each instance, however, the prophecies come to pass: fate proved stronger than diverting actions taken in the light of foreknowledge provided by the oracle.[20] So too for Cassandra, a tragic figure in Greek mythology, for whom the gift of clairvoyance had been delivered as a curse: no one would listen to her warnings or believe her prophecies. Thus she forewarned in vain of the fall of Troy and the trick with the wooden horse. She even foresaw the details of her own and Agamemnon's murder. Yet she was unable to avert the course of destiny, helpless in the face of her own foreseen demise.[21] In all these stories the message is clear: knowing the future does not necessarily help you to alter your destiny. What distinguished Greek oracles from the prophets of ancient Egypt, the Bible and Nordic myths was that the prophetic gift of the former had been transferred from gods to people in possession of special hallucinogenic powers.

The Druids of ancient Celtic cultures, who were equally renowned for their powers of divination, drew on different sources and powers. As Danah Zohar notes, Celtic Druids were able to read the future from 'the flights of birds, from the shape of clouds or tree roots, with the aid of bone-divining (using the boiled-clean right shoulder blade of an animal) or from rowan sticks'.[22] Merlin, renowned as the greatest wizard of all, foresaw many of the significant turning points in the life of King Arthur and far beyond that. His prophecies and predictions cover the crusades as well as the reign of James I, Henry VIII and Richard the Lionheart who lived some seven hundred years later. Merlin prophesied that:

> The Lionheart will against the Saracens rise,
> And purchase from him many a glorious prize . . .
> But whilst abroad these great acts shall be done,
> All things at home shall to disorder run.
> Coop'ed up and cage'd the Lion then shall be,
> But after suffrance ransom'd and set free.
> . . . Last by a poisonous shaft, the Lion die.[23]

While Merlin was the most famous of the Celtic sages, his fellow druids were said to have been equally accomplished in the foreknowledge of the future, a task they performed without recourse to hallucinogenic or hypnotic aids.

The Book of Changes, the *I Ching*, finally, is one of the few divinatory traditions that has survived for some four thousand years without losing any of its pertinence.[24] Throughout this time, the *I Ching* has been consulted by individuals seeking guidance about decisions at crucial moments in their lives. The *I Ching* is rooted in Taoism, Tao meaning *the way that is in harmony with the moment in time*. It locates the questioner in a wider context that transcends the particular time and space of the consultation. It places chance and the quality of the moment at the centre of its system of meanings. As Carl Gustav Jung explains in his introduction to the *I Ching*,

> The matter of interest seems to be the configuration formed by chance events in the moment of observation . . .
> .   .   .
> Synchronicity takes the coincidence of events in space and time as meaning something more than mere chance, namely, a peculiar interdependence of objective events among themselves as well as with the subjective (psychic) state of the observer.[25]

In the *I Ching*, the quality of the moment, the projective situation, the inner state and the consciousness of the person asking the question are placed into the wider scheme of cosmic connectedness in which every unique event is seen as interdependent with every other unique event. Thus coincidence, interdependence, connectivity and uniqueness are the key components that work the magic of this particular system of divination.

Reading patterns, recognizing significant coincidences, understanding synchronicity and establishing acausal connections are means to unlock the future that are in fact shared across history by people with special access to the future: by Druids and Nordic sages, astrologers, as well as individuals consulting the *I Ching*. The principles on which these divinations are based, we need to appreciate further, are diametrically opposed to those underpinning scientific prediction, the primary and socially most legitimated means of modern Western cultures to access the unknowable future.[26] In contrast to these ancient practices, scientific prediction is wedded to the principle of linear causality and projects into the future past patterns of repetition. Despite the fact that scientists were trespassing on a terrain that was the exclusive preserve of God, scientific prediction gained acceptance from the Church on the basis that it merely brought together knowledge about processes that have occurred in the past and are therefore expected to continue into the future. That is to say, given that the past rather than the future was the source of its prowess, the Church did not consider that predictive science was blasphemous or the work of Satan.

More recently, the substantial unintended consequences of innovative technologies have shown the past-based predictions of science to be inadequate to the task of foretelling potential impacts and consequences of the adoption and application of those technologies. In these instances, the scientifically known past is proving an inappropriate guide to action. The massive indeterminacies that accompany technologies from nuclear power to fridges have taken centre-stage, where they pose major problems for a system of divination that requires a large number of certainties and knowledge of the precise initial conditions before any statistical and probabilistic predictions can be made. Interconnectedness, interdependence and seemingly acausal connections place this eminent and hugely successful system under pressure: climate change and global warming, increasing floods and major fires, and human health hazards arising from the global application of innovative technologies are all phenomena where extensive knowledge of the past is no longer sufficient to predict the future with certainty or accuracy.

Where the *predictions* fall far short of what is expected of science, the scientific capacity to *create* futures through intended and unintended consequences of its inventions, in contrast, far outstrips expectations. This is a distinction that needs to be teased out and its paradoxical relations understood with reference to each other. The first thing to note is that the cultural and technological creation *of* futures could never be mapped neatly on to the quests for knowledge *about* the future. Despite their obvious interdependence, both cultural practices developed along largely divergent temporal paths. Thus, for example, lack of foreknowledge about weather and seasonal variation facilitated particular agricultural practices that secured the future by growing a wide variety of crops and keeping an extensive range of animals so that failure in one part of the system could be offset by stability and success in other parts of it. Similarly, not being able to predict drought and crop failure encouraged the saving of grain and seed for several years ahead so that bad seasons could be bridged with grain and seed from the stores. These practices in no way aided the predictive capacity of the societies concerned, but instead created long-term food security through practice: survival through lean and catastrophic years into an extended future was secured through foresight and precaution rather than prediction.

In industrial societies this temporal relation seems to have been reversed. Monocultures, economies of scale and chemical assistance make an increase in productivity predictable but reduce long-term food safety and security. Increase in predictability over the short term is traded against long-term certainty that the future fertility of the land is secured and ensured. Looking at a specific example we can note how increased control over the extended present through the use of fertilizers and pesticides has not increased the predictability of the future but has, instead, vastly increased the unforeseen long-term impacts on the land in question as well as all living creatures of this earth. For example, none of us – humans, fish or fowl – are safe from endocrine disrupters that have worked their way up the food chain, nor are our descendents and successor generations safe from their long-term impacts. A similar relation pertains between knowledge of and the creation of a nuclear future. Efforts to secure energy for a medium-term future resulted in largely unplanned and unpredicted long-term radiation that predetermines not just our health and that of our children but the health and future presents of successor generations for millennia.

The quest to *know* the future therefore needs to be understood in relation to and in distinction from the cultural *creation* of the future. Much of the latter will still occupy us in chapter 6. At this point we need to return to time-transcending practices that date back to the earliest phases of cultural development. In the next section, therefore, we focus on cultural responses to mortality and impermanence.

Creating Immortality and Permanence

In response to mortality, our earliest ancestors constructed their being eternally.[27] They conceived of an afterlife, a life after death. Confronted with impermanence they created permanence by a variety of means: through burial and ritual, things and representations, myth and heroism, belief systems and institutions. With burial of their dead our earliest ancestors transcended their allotted time on earth. Burial ensured safe journey to the world of ancestors and created social continuity across generations. Heroism, in contrast, made life worth living. It extended a person's existence beyond their grave, their deeds to be sung and told for many generations, their lives elevated as shining examples to their successors. With the production of artefacts, knowledge was not just objectified and externalized but it survived into the following generations, thus loosening the dependence on co-presence for knowledge to circulate. Many cultural constructions and creations endured for tens of thousands of years to be marvelled at by us today: burial chambers and stone circles, tools and pottery, cave paintings and written texts, jewellery and mathematical spheres carved from stone. Belief systems, finally, provided comforting responses to ontological fears and insecurities, while political institutions ensured the continuity of the collective beyond the bounded existence of their individual members. I have restricted the focus here to responses to death and, in the light of this choice, selected burial, religion and the creation of things as examples to illustrate the point.

Impermanent are all created things but underlying them is an eternal atemporal reality. This is the shared belief that underpins all the major religions,[28] where the principle of infinity and timelessness is variably called Brahman, Nirvana, Absolute Tao, Yahweh, God and Allah. Irrespective of how the world is conceived – in terms of cycles of reincarnation or rebirth, of absolute flux rooted in the continuous flow of creation and destruction, as apparent and absolute aspects of the Absolute Tao, as creation with a beginning and an end or as irreversible progress towards increasing perfection – the purpose of the earthly journey is reunification with the eternal ultimate reality, however this may be defined. Despite their considerable diversity, therefore, the world religions – Hinduism, Buddhism, Taoism, Judaism, Christianity and Islam – share a belief in an eternal, transcendent principle beyond time and space from which our world emanates and to which we are ultimately to return. The cosmologies and respective paths to salvation may differ, but underlying that divergence is a common vision of the transcendent eternal.

Subtle differences characterize time in the major spiritual traditions of the East. Hinduism, the oldest of the major religions, which is complex and diverse, has undergone many changes until today we can identify six schools of thought, each with its own cosmology, implicit theory of time, and path to salvation. Yet in all its schools and branches the Hindu universe is conceived as an *impermanent* manifestation of Brahman, the atemporal source of all being, to which we are ultimately to return in timescales measured in millions of years.[29] Moksha is the aspired release from the endless cycles of karmic reincarnation where all actions of past lives are taken into consideration and influence the forms of life in which one is reincarnated. Ultimate salvation, therefore, is the unification with Atman, the spirit of Brahman.

For Buddhists the liberation from the endless cycles of birth, death and suffering is Nirvana. In the manifest world of interconnected and interdependent consciousness, every thought and action contributes to a whole that reaches back into a past without beginning and forward into a future without end. The enduring self is an illusion: there is no doer, only the deed.[30] It is these past deeds that condition the level and form of each rebirth. Nothing, however, is handed on in the transaction, not even the soul. What unites the many different branches of Buddhism with their different interpretations of what aspect of time is real is the eightfold path to Nirvana. This path to Enlightenment involves overcoming the transience of existence, its pleasures, pains, anxieties and comforts. Through the abandonment of time, Self, conceptual thought and all desire, the aspired state of deathlessness can be achieved.

Taoism, the third of the major spiritual systems of the East, holds a similar position on transience. It assumes that timelessness is the fundamental reality below change, that change emanates from this atemporal wholeness. Change and non-change, time and timelessness are a unified whole. In Taoism it is recognized that every action causes a reaction and all extreme positions revert to their opposites. Finding the path of least resistance and to return a negative force with a positive one – hatred with virtue, evil with good – are therefore general guides to practical means to Tao, the way and centre. The statement 'Do nothing and everything will be done' falls into place when we understand the role of time in Tao as both substance and process of the Absolute Tao, the nameless mysterious essence of Non-Being that pervades nature.

In the Judeo-Christian and Islamic religions the transcendental is not just named but also personified. Yahweh, God and Allah are beyond and outside time. They are source, creator and owner of time and all things temporal.[31] In the development of each of these religions, deeds and critical moments are located in time, remembered and celebrated. Their respective histories have an unrepeatable beginning and an irrevocable end, a moment of creation and a time of final judgement, all of which are in the hands of their own God. The focus of life on earth is directed towards the future: the coming of the Messiah, the second coming of Christ, the Day of Judgement. Goodman writes with respect to Islam: 'Time in the Koran is the precarious moral span of history suspended between judgement and creation. Here we act and choose and are tested, with results that endure through eternity.'[32] Deeds in this life, therefore, will count on judgement day when everyone is called to account.

Thus, whether embedded in an eschatology of salvation or a quest for liberation from the infinite cycles of rebirth and reincarnation, in every case the ultimate religious goal is to connect with the eternal, with the realm beyond time.

This quest for the eternal realm beyond time and death does not, however, originate from the major religions. Rather, its emergence is much older and can be traced to the very beginning of human cultural existence. Archaeological evidence is amassing from across the world which suggests that funerary rites took place at the dawn of humanity. These rites, which accompanied burial, assisted the deceased on their journey to the otherworld. In the Shanidar caves of Iraq, human remains have been found together with evidence that the person had been buried on a bed of flowers. The bones are thought to be 60,000 years old, suggesting that at the time of Neanderthal Man people already took part in rituals when they buried their dead. In south-eastern Australia ancient remains were discovered that indicated burial and a form of ancestor worship. These remains were dated at 30,000 years old. Across Europe burial sites are registered from the early Neolithic period onwards.[33] Burial mounds and burial chambers housing mass graves as well as graves containing single persons are suggestive of beliefs in existence after death, creating continuity in the face of finality. In particular, archaeological records suggest that bones of the deceased were circulating as a means to ensure continuity across generations through physical ties with the dead. As Gosden argues with reference to evidence provided by Barrett, Bradley and Green:[34]

> From this viewpoint, the earlier Neolithic is seen to be dominated by a series of rituals transforming the dead into ancestral figures. Reference to ancestors is thought to be the means by which access to land and resources was negotiated. Human bones played a central role in a complex series of rituals and appear to have been moved across the landscape many times before they were finally buried.[35]

In ancient Egypt the resurrection of Osiris to life in the underworld promised survival after death, that is, it guaranteed eternal life to the deceased, so long as their relatives did for them what Isis did for Osiris, so long as they re-enacted the prescribed rituals *ab origine*. Initially this applied only to royals, but later it became instituted more widely within Egyptian society. In Africa, the belief in death as departure to another life rather than annihilation has survived to this day. The body decays but the spirit moves on to join the ancestors in the realm beyond time to continue life much as she or he had lived it in their community of the living. John Mbiti explains how some of the words associated with death imply a pilgrimage, a journey to the 'real' home in the thereafter and how the dead are buried with food and possessions to sustain them on this perilous journey across the river of death that separates the two worlds.[36] Belief system and practice interweave to construct individual and collective being eternally.

Given this extensive evidence of the transcendental constitution of life and the eternal as source and destiny of all that is temporal, it would be surprising if members of archaic and ancient cultures had not also sought to create the eternal on earth as an integral part of their finite lives. In the earlier part of this chapter I have already outlined the eternal principle with reference to megalithic temples and the creation of the perfect circle. These structures embodied archetypal number systems that encode a highly sophisticated knowledge of geometry, usually credited to the philosophers of ancient Greece. What Plato put into the following words, 'Every diagram, system of numbers, every scheme of harmony, every law of the movement of the stars, ought to appear one to him who studies rightly',[37] found expression in the temple structures and artefacts of Celtic and Nordic cultures of the Neolithic.

Numbers are atemporal and carry symbolic significance. As such they are ideally placed to unify heaven and earth, the eternal and the temporal, existence and experience. Numbers give access to patterns and facilitate their reproduction. Patterns can only be perceived by standing outside time since they freeze and hold still what is moving and transient. An example would be the patterns created by the movement of stars over time. However, we need to appreciate that the geometry of the Neolithic was not an abstract enterprise. Rather, it was performed and practised: externalized in myth and ritual, art and artefacts, temple structures and the underground arrangements of burial mounds.

I will use the carved stone spheres of Neolithic Britain to illustrate the wider argument.[38] The architect Keith Critchlow describes these objects as 'beautiful and precise solid geometrical figures, veritable works of art carved in stone'.[39] They were made of granite, which means that they will have taken months to create, given that at that time the tools too would have been made from stone. Clearly the permanence of the artefacts' material was chosen as appropriate to the eternal mathematical principles involved. The spheres' geometric compositions expressed the symmetry and regularity of the 'major archetypal division of the unitary sphere':[40] octahedral, tetrahedral, dodecahedral, icosahedral, cuboctahedral, icosidodecahedral (the latter two being combinations of two geometric sphere shapes superimposed upon each other to reveal fourteen and thirty-two faces respectively). Analysis of the spheres' geometry revealed special emphasis on the numbers five, seven and nine, which are known to hold a special place in archaic and ancient cultures the world over.

These hand-sized material expressions of atemporal geometry were carved some one thousand years before the insights of Pythagoras and the writings of Plato in ancient Greece.[41] The atemporal realm of ideas and number, attributed to Plato, was thus predated by at least a millennium in the geometry of these Neolithic artefacts. This is not surprising, given that the pervasive beliefs in an eternal ground of being reach back to the beginning of humanity, and that, as a general principle, practice tends to predate written expression. Belief, practice and performance, I want to argue, create an eternal braid of transience and eternity that is woven into the very fabric of archaic and ancient cultures and their material expressions.

Modifying Nature's Times and Rhythms

To light the hours of darkness, to provide a stable food supply through periods of seasonal and climatic variation, to keep ageing and decay at bay, all are cultural means to alter nature's transience and rhythms. The details may differ between peoples and phases of history, but the basic impulse is shared across time and space: it is the human endeavour to impose a cultural will on time. Equally, to dance and make music, to write fiction or produce a film involves an active engagement with time, whether this be through particular rhythms, through changes in the relation between past, present and future, or through technological means to edit events into new constellations. The point here is not the detail of practices but explication of the different time-transcending principles involved in the various cultural practices and performances.

The creation of light for the times and places of darkness and the production of warmth for cold periods and spaces were key technological achievements of our earliest ancestors. No wonder then that the way people obtained fire is told in myths across cultures and historical periods. What those myths share is the understanding that fire belonged to the gods and was not easily relinquished by them. Fire came into human possession through theft or trickery and its acquisition required the help of non-human friends. In Greek mythology, Prometheus was punished severely by the gods for giving fire to the mortals, and in an Amerindian myth from British Columbia many animals lost their lives when Coyote stole what belonged to the gods.[42]

Initially, fire would have been harnessed before it was controlled. It would have been tended and maintained long before there were technological means to transport it. Archaeological evidence suggests the cultural use of fire since Peking Man, that is, for hundreds of thousands of years. At that time, fire would have provided warmth during the cold period, light during the hours of darkness and safety from predators. Not until the Neolithic period, however, that is, around 4000 BC, is there archaeological evidence of the capacity to create fire and with it all the dramatic changes that flowed from it. The records suggest that the production of fire is implicated in the very beginning of agriculture, in domestic changes associated primarily with the growing and preserving of food, and it is a precondition for the creation of metal tools and objects.

Closer to our own time, central heating has changed the design of houses, clothing habits in winter, the organization of family life and the interior layout of homes. A similar story of changes in culture can be told with the history of electric light. It banished darkness not just in houses but in the streets and allowed for the division between day and night to become blurred, producing virtual interchangeability between them, and with it facilitating the 24/7, non-stop society. It engendered the shift of work and pleasure activities from daytime to night-time. From fire to candles and electricity, we can therefore say, each of the particular temporal alterations changed social relations and cultural practices.

If we look at preservation practices, whether these are concerned with food or bodies, we can again discern a clear desire to impose the cultural will on time, to arrest change and ageing. Let us consider food preservation to illustrate the point. The burying of food, which is one of the earliest methods of preservation, encodes important temporal knowledge about the interaction of air and living matter, that is, about the corrosive effect of air on matter. The application of this knowledge results in the conservation and preservation of food through the exclusion of air, using burial in soil or ice or, in more modern times, bottling and freezing. Preservation through drying, in contrast, is based on knowledge about the interaction of water, air and living matter, and the recognition that in this combination water is a central component in the process of decay. Therefore the extraction of water – be it through heat, smoke or wind – can keep decay at bay. In some cases of dried foods (pasta, rice and pulses, for example) the process of decay can be arrested for indefinite periods.

With modern methods of preservation such as freezing, irradiation and genetic modification, the desire to arrest change and processes of ageing becomes dependent on ever more complex temporal relations and technological aids, involving electricity, nuclear power and biotechnology. Let us take the genetic modification of food as an exemplar. On the one hand, genetic modification is preceded by and rests on millennia of breeding technologies and three hundred years of academic biological science. On the other hand, it dramatically departs from both. Conventional breeding is achieved through changes in the phenotype. It depends on cross-breeding within species across generations. Genetic modification, in contrast, cuts out the generational waiting game by carrying out the breeding operation at the level of the individual gene, that is the genotype rather than the phenotype. The waiting involved, therefore, is now not across the generations of animals and plants but relates to the laboratory trials, given that, in principle at least, the change is instantaneous – it happens in one specimen in the present. Moreover, unlike conventional breeding techniques, genetic modification is not constrained by the species barrier. To transcend that barrier it taps into the genetic material that is shared by all species. It thus extends its scientific reach to the beginning of time. At the other end of the temporal spectrum, outcomes are open-ended. They potentially stretch to the end of time. Given its extraordinary temporal reach, especially its capacity to construct unknowable future presents for untold successor generations, it is not surprising that this particular effort to impose a cultural will on change is encountering such strong public resistance.

Just very briefly I also want to mention temporal practices that create cultural rhythms, sequences and duration. Again, despite the richness of this hugely fascinating subject matter, it is not so much the detail as the general principles that concern us here. According to Mircea Eliade, music and especially dances were first performed to reactualize an 'archetypal gesture or commemorate a mythical moment'.[43] The choreography and rhythms of the dances had models outside the profanity of everyday life. Thus a ritual performance may re-enact a dance or song first performed by a god, to evoke the magic necessary for a successful endeavour, or to 'assure good order in the cosmos'. Rhythmicity, such an integral part of nature's temporality, is fashioned to cultural need and desire irrespective of where and when a dance or song is recreated and performed.

A similar temporal structure, it seems, applies to narrative. Telling stories, people have altered the sequence and duration of events since time immemorial, even when the stories told have remained largely unchanged over generations. Writing merely extended this capacity to creatively rearrange the relations between past, present and future, and with film this ability was taken to previously unimaginable heights.[44] In film, duration, pace and chronology are open to restructuring: to compression and expansion, repositioning and revision, modification and amplification. Thus rhythmicity and the past, present and future are culturally malleable whatever the chosen means for telling a story. Even if the precise form differs between modes, historical periods and specific performances, temporality becomes amenable to 'editing'.

Superimposing Phases and Social Structure

So far we have been concerned primarily with responses to death, finitude, transience and rhythmicity. In this last section of the chapter we focus on the practices associated with the structuring by cultural means of the life cycle and the temporality of mundane life, that is, rites of passage, festivals and the calendar system.

'Rites of passage', a term coined by the anthropologist Arnold van Gennep,[45] are cultural markers in the cycle of life, key staging posts that are superimposed on the lived continuum. Rites of passage assist all participants in their move from one socially defined phase of life into another. Often they help us separate the sacred from the profane elements of our lifeworld and embed us in frameworks of meaning. Most societies have means to mark some of the key stations of their members' lives. They welcome and integrate new children into the community, where the children may be baptized or circumcised or purified over the smoke of the Konkerberry tree. There may be special celebrations when children begin their education, enter the Buddhist temple for their period of instruction, take first communion, become one with the crocodile spirit, or leave the house of the women to enter their age set. During the onset of puberty and adolescence they may have to undergo trials of strength and bravery, be subjected to initiation rites or be publicly introduced to society. Marriage too is celebrated the world over with culturally distinct rituals. In many societies, furthermore, the end of working life is ritually marked and celebrated. Funerary rites, finally, allow for communal expression of grief, provide guides for conduct of the bereaved during periods of maximum chaos and emotional upheaval, and they specify correct procedures to assist the dead on their journey to the afterlife, the realms of the ancestors or the living dead.

According to van Gennep, rites of passage themselves have a distinct structure, which may involve some or all of the following features: separation from society, a liminal phase between the old and the new, and reintegration into the community with a new status. They entail departure, becoming and transformation. Ritual death and spiritual rebirth, therefore, are the symbolisms that underpin many of these celebrated changes from one social status to another.

A very different cultural punctuation of the continuum of socio-environmental existence is activated and achieved with religious and social festivals. These impose a social structure on the annual rhythms of seasons, moons and tides. They provide the collective beat that facilitates communal life, be this with the extended family, the clan, the local community, worshippers of a particular church, or members of a political organization. In the weekly and daily cycle those socially imposed markers – opening and closing times, the beginning and end of the school day, weekdays and weekends – structure the everyday and make provision for family time. Even in the contemporary 24/7, non-stop society where these markers are as far as possible erased, the socially constituted distinctions continue to hold. The weekend, for example, is still marked off from weekdays in its social and economic status, as evidenced by the fact that weekend work is remunerated differently from weekday work during 'normal' working hours. In addition, the tax year and the budgetary cycle structure the economic year, while the election cycle frames and delimits much of political activity. This imposition of the social will, this structuring to cultural design, weaves an intricate temporal fabric of interdependent cycles within cycles within cycles that connects societies and distinguishes them from each other. While the stations in the life cycle are relative to the persons and age sets involved, the collective structuring, both sacred and profane, is tied to an external time which provides an objective framework for timing that can be shared across societies and generations.

I think it is safe to say that nothing in the cosmos, and no living system in nature, repeats without variation. If it did, it would be a sign of death, since without variation there is no change, without change there is no growth and development, and without growth and development, finally, there is no life.

It is the human endeavour, as I have argued throughout this chapter, which imposes *in*variability on the changing world. Invariability, therefore, is the mark of culture that we find in the stone circles and temples, in the carved geometric spheres and the theories of Plato, in myth and ritual practice. It is the search for transcendence, immortality and the eternal in the face of transience, finitude and change that moves the human spirit to its greatest achievements. The awareness of finitude, the conscious search for transcendence, and the construction of immutability need therefore to be conceptualized as culturally coeval.

INTERLUDE

BODY TIME, CLOCK TIME, SOCIAL TIME

Body Time
is being and becoming
is birth and death, growth and ageing
is all of past and future gathered up in the present
is rhythmic repetition with variation: invariability is death
is re/production, regeneration and repair/healing
is temporality, timing, tempo, intensity
is finite and transcendent
is contextual
is life

Clock Time
is linear and spatial
is decontextualized and quantified
is counting oscillations represented by number
is repetition of the same irrespective of when and where
is invariable – variation means clock going wrong
is creation of time to human design
is product, money and profit
is infinitely divisible
is artefact

Social Time
is body and clock time
is performed and constructed
is repetition with and without variation
is reproduction, regeneration and regulation
is all of past and future gathered up in the present
is structure, temporality, timing, tempo and rhythmicity
is history and biography, memory and anticipation
is irreversible, contextual and abstract
is process, product and measure
is finite and transcendent
is exchange value
is negotiated

5

In Pursuit of Time Know-how

In mythology, as we have seen in previous chapters, there is a time before temporality. This is the world before night and day, before birth and death, growth and decay. It is the dream time of womb and darkness and everlasting soft light. It is paradise, the realm of origin and innocence, of consciousness without the I, of embeddedness and unity with the whole.[1] Time emerges from this unity in dualistic form: light and dark, night and day; being and non-being, birth and death; warm and cold, summer and winter, wet and dry, flooding and drought. Repeating cycles become recognizable patterns. Naming and numbering these repetitions makes them predictable, allows for anticipation and planning, creates a sense of ownership and control. Not surprisingly, therefore, time know-how was first developed at the behest of sovereigns and applied with their approval.

In this chapter we look at this naming and numbering. We are moving away from cultural efforts to transcend the temporal boundaries and inexorabilities set by nature and focus instead on the quest for special skills associated with the knowledge of time, that is, the pursuit of time know-how. Know-how implies in-order-to knowledge, knowledge for use, that is, knowledge to structure, order and synchronize social life, to regulate it and inculcate time discipline. It encompasses useful knowledge, knowledge to maintain and enhance power, be it the sovereign's, the church's or employers' power. In this chapter on the search for time know-how, we trace a number of the moves towards ownership and control. We explore measurement and prediction through a range of calendar systems, standard and world time on the basis of clock time and the development of instantaneity and simultaneity through electronic communication.

Towards the end of the chapter we reflect on how historians and social scientists make sense of the social relations of time, of the historical developments, of differences and similarities in approaches, and of the complex ways the past features in the present. We consider a range of conceptual tools with their accompanying effects and ask whether or not some times and temporal relations might be preferable to others. In the last section of this chapter, then, we look back and begin to relate the diverse approaches to each other. We then use the way of looking and understanding promoted in these pages and explicated in the final section of this chapter to guide us through the last chapter on industrial societies' quest for the control of time.

Reckoning Time

Time cannot be thought about without the processes by which we divide and measure it, wrote Émile Durkheim in *The Elementary Forms of Religious Life*. He was not alone in holding this view. As I showed in chapter 2, some of the most prominent philosophers of ancient Greece suggested much the same, as did numerous contemporary social scientists engaged with the social relations of time.[2] Time, they thought, was inescapably tied to counting, naming and numbering the succession of units of years, months, weeks, days and their subdivisions. For social theorists this activity is inescapably social. It has its root in social organization and synchronization, and in the need to anticipate, plan and regulate collective existence. The diversity of means to track, express and represent the same rhythmic phenomena certainly testifies to that assertion. At the same time, however, the dualism of natural and cultural time as cosmic and social phenomena does not aid or advance our understanding.

Clearly, without the cosmic rounds there would be no quest to number and name the cycles; without cultures affected and challenged by the phenomena there would be no culturally distinct representation. The cycles of the sun, moon and planets exist whether or not humans are challenged by them or seek to appropriate them.

The interpretations, representations and models, in contrast, are dependent on there being such phenomena to be known, named and appropriated in the first place. That is to say, time reckoning is dependent on there being regular recurrent phenomena that can be counted and numbered: be they cosmic, biological or sociocultural. Thus, to Norbert Elias,

> The calendar's unrepeatable succession of numbered years symbolically represents the unrepeatable of social and natural events. It thus serves as a means of orientation in the great continuum of change which is at once the natural and the social world.
> . . .
> Not 'people' and 'nature' as two separate entities but 'people in nature' is the basic concept which is needed . . .[3]

Elias's work directs us to the great integrating capacity that is the precondition to any kind of time reckoning. In it Elias posits a fifth reflective dimension (in addition to the three of space and one of time) that incorporates the synthesizing process in the analysis. Elias's conceptual approach to the issue of time reckoning is the one taken here. The traditional dualism of natural and social time is abandoned in favour of a more reflective and reflexive, synthesizing perspective on the subject matter.

Archaeological and historical records suggest that cultural structuring of social life with reference to cosmic and natural phenomena dates back to prehistoric times. In Britain and France this relates to Neolithic stone structures and burrows that were erected some three to four thousand years ago. In ancient Egypt and Babylonia, India and China, the beginnings of time reckoning have to be sought several thousand years before that. In all cases there emerges a tight, culturally based unity between cosmos, nature, the divine, and social organization. For Neolithic cultures of Britain and France, leaving no written records, the social role and function can only be inferred from archaeological records. For ancient cultures with written records – Babylonian and Egyptian, Chinese and Indian, Maya, Inca and Aztec, for example – the fragments of records become more a question of interpretation and less one of inference and conjecture. Moreover, despite the vast differences in culture, time and place, and irrespective of whether the moon, the sun or the stars were the primary source of structuring, there were stunning similarities between reckoning systems and cumulative cycle building that resulted in social accounting systems based on astronomically large numbers.[4]

A whole new discipline emerged with the study of the relation of ancient buildings to cosmic phenomena. Archaeoastronomy is the study of alignments of architecture, landscape and heavenly bodies.[5] It starts from the assumption that the interest in cosmic rhythms has influenced human development right from the beginning of social life and that we can discern this engagement and effort to establish a temporal order in the buildings surviving from ancient cultures. The argument, based on archaeological records from Britain, South America and the Middle East, is that buildings were aligned with the stars so as to bring into unity heaven and earth, social organization and the divine. The rising and setting of heavenly bodies was tracked and fixed against features in the landscape and the extreme positions of sun, moon and planets aligned with respect to the local horizon and key features of buildings. Thus solstice and equinox, the moon cycle extremes which repeat every 18.61 years and the disappearance and reappearance of stars have all been related to ancient structures as distant in time and space as the pyramids and temples of ancient Egypt, the temple structures of Inca, Maya and Aztec cultures, and the stone circles, long burrows and cromlechs of Neolithic Britain.

The work on this unity of planetary motion, horizon features and buildings dates back to the late nineteenth century. In 1894 Sir J. Norman Lockyer published findings that suggested that the origin of astronomy and the calendar were to be sought in the orientation of buildings to significant cosmic events. On the basis of his extensive studies of Egyptian temples and pyramids Lockyer proposed that every aspect of the buildings, from walls and doorways to axes, was constructed so as to stand in a deliberate, oriented relation to the rising and setting of the sun and significant stars such as Venus and Sirius whose annual re-emergence coincided with the flooding of the Nile. During the 1930s Alexander Thom studied the megalithic sites of Britain and concluded similarly that the geometry and metrology of the builders of these structures was developed to such an advanced level that there could be no doubt that the holders of such knowledge were capable of keeping lunar and solar time. From the construction of the structures, their sites and their orientation Thom discerned Pythagorean geometry several thousand years before Pythagoras, and knowledge of planetary cycles that, until then, tended to be associated exclusively with the high cultures of the Middle East, the Orient and the Americas.[6] The buildings pinpoint the moon's 18.61 year cycle and suggest a calendar system of eight or sixteen equal months, established with reference to the horizon positions of the rising and setting sun.

This and similar archaeoastronomical work was criticized by archaeologists who insisted that intention and astronomical knowledge must not be read into these structures without corroboration from other sources. The research was accused of imposing contemporary knowledge on the surviving fragments of these ancient cultures. Today, the distance between the various disciplines involved is narrowing and collaboration rather than boundary demarcations is prevalent, bringing together work that has developed along separate paths. While there is still substantial disagreement about the detail of interpretation, there is broad agreement on the alignment thesis, on the special significance of the moon for the earliest structures dating from 4000 to 1500 BC and on a subsequent shift in orientations towards the sun. Evidence from across the world suggests that the moon was the earliest planetary source of cultural forms of time reckoning and associated rhythmic practices that integrated all the significant levels of existence. Orientation to the sun seems to have been a later development.

This change in emphasis from moon to sun, noted in archaeoastronomy and archaeology, seems to coincide with changes in the relation to death and treatment of the dead.

With respect to Neolithic Britain, for example, it appears to correspond to a change in practice related to the bones of deceased members, which the records suggest have been circulating widely among the different cultural sites. At about the same time that buildings began to be oriented towards the sun's movements, bones ceased to circulate as currency and markers of identity and stayed buried instead with the skeleton intact.[7]

According to the sociologist Eviator Zerubavel, the calendar is the first institution through which cultures established and maintained temporal regularity.[8] From the above we can see, however, that this assertion needs some qualification as well as more detailed understanding of what a calendar might be, given the enormous historical and contextual variation. Are we, for example, to understand oriented buildings, of the types outlined above, as calendar systems or should we consider them mere precursors to something more tightly delimited? Since there are no definite boundaries which would allow unambiguous classification, I prefer an inclusive approach that allows for the widest possible interpretation.

Zerubavel's functional perspective on the matter of time reckoning can be traced back to the writings of Durkheim, who suggested that: 'A calendar expresses the rhythm of the collective activities, while at the same time its function is to assure regularity.'[9] Clearly, social coordination, synchronization and temporal regulation need to be located in a temporal framework that transcends the specific society, in something bigger than the society that is employing temporal know-how to organize its life in time and space. However, the kinds of similarities and differences we find in calendar systems, past and present, across the world are reducible neither to representations of differences in social organization nor to social function. That is to say, neither are explanations for why and on what basis Mayan and Aztec societies, for example, shared with ancient Sumerian, Babylonian, Egyptian, Indian and Chinese cultures an astronomical understanding that was rooted in a sexagesimal number system, while arriving at very different answers to account for the 'five extra days' that could not be fitted into their cycles of 360 days for the year, 12 months and 4 units of 6 hours per day. They give us no clue as to why European and

Middle Eastern cultures might have attempted to combine primarily moon and sun cycles while Mesoamerican cultures sought to construct calendar systems of extraordinary complexity, combining a ritual calendar of 260 days with the cycles of sun, Venus, moon and additional other cycles such as a nine-day week linked to gods associated with the night.

A third strong assertion, proffered by sociologists and a number of anthropologists, is that sacred and profane times are irreducibly distinct.[10] Again, it was Durkheim who first insisted on this division.[11] He went so far as to suggest that the social category of time arose with the religious need to differentiate between the sacred and profane. The most extensive substantiation of this assertion is offered by Zerubavel's extended discussion in *Hidden Rhythms* about the Jewish Sabbath in relation to the Jewish and Christian calendar and the irreducible separation between sacred and profane activities in Jewish life. While there are clearly many compelling cases where these categorical distinctions apply, they provide no basis from which to generalize across cultures past and present. The specific template in conjunction with the categorical distinction of sacred and profane close off the analysis to other modes of religious being such as Buddhism and Hinduism, which unified the sacred and profane in practice, or Mayan and early Egyptian cultures that sought to integrate the realms of heaven and earth through ritual. I wonder whether it is the cultural location of sociologists and anthropologists together with their modernist conceptual tools that engender such narrow social interpretations of what are hugely diverse and complex cultural traditions.

Let me outline some of the key features of the Mayan calendar, most of which had been shared by their neighbours and Mesoamerican predecessors, in order to qualify some of these conventional social science assertions.[12] To locate Mayan culture historically and spatially, we need to know that the earliest recorded Mayan villages date back to some 1000 years BC. The last Mayan kingdom was conquered by Spanish invading forces in 1697. The classic period of Mayan culture spanned from about 300 to 900 AD. At the height of Mayan power the territory extended from Guatemala and Belize to Western Honduras, El Salvador and lower Mexico. Earliest records of the Mayan ritual calendar system are dated variably between around 700 to 500 BC. To appreciate the intimate connection between time, astronomy, religion and sociocultural activity we need to know that 'day', 'sun' and 'feast' are the multiple meanings associated with *k'in*, the word for time, and that *ah k'in* means priest, the keeper of time. The major achievement of the Mayan calendar system was to combine into a single unity a number of incompatible cycles – ritual and planetary, including the sun, Venus and the moon – each important not only in its own right but also in its relation to all the other cycles. This hugely complex system allowed the keepers of time to determine festival periods, auspicious and unlucky days as well as right and wrong times for specified activities. It enabled them to forecast eclipses, conceived as periods of great danger, and it legitimated them, finally, as keepers of a collective memory, which tied the present to mythological times of origin and temporally located significant historical events.

The Maya's earliest recorded calendar system is the ritual cycle which comprised 20 units of 13 days which were numbered and 13 units of 20 days which were represented by symbols (mostly animal) to culminate in a sacred round of 260 days (also roughly the timespan from conception to birth, which is, according to modern medicine, 266 days). This ritual cycle was meshed with the solar cycle, which was called the vague year because its 365.2422 days were recognized to drift over long periods of time. The solar year was subdivided into 18 months of 20 days plus 5 unlucky days that were considered to be outside the year. The combination of ritual and solar cycles arrived at unique dates over a period of 52 years, which were made up of 73 × 260 ritual days and 52 × 365 solar days. The ritual and solar rounds were further integrated with the cycle of Venus, which repeated every 584 days; 8 solar years were equivalent to 5 Venus cycles. Combined into a larger round of 104 solar years, 65 Venus and 146 ritual cycles, these incompatible rhythms could be synchronized and unified.

To fix important dates in an absolute chronology, lunar cycles were included to provide supplementary information about temporal location. Deities and heavenly bodies, religion and history, daily practice and mythical past were thus brought into a coherent whole in this calendar system which operated routinely with dates and numbers extending to five digits and more. Here the sacred is implicated in the profane and vice versa. The explicated always includes that which is not the explicit focus of attention. Physical phenomena are suffused with the spirit world of deities and demons. Ritual practice is implicated in bureaucratic regulation. Administrative practices are in tune with ritual prerequisites. In their mutual implication all the components of this multiplex time reckoning system constitute the historically and contextually unique cultural system.

Despite the fact that all societies had at their disposal the same physical data of moon, sun and stars from which to construct their systems of time reckoning, there were tremendous differences between the knowledge systems. These were particularly marked at the extreme ends of the temporal scale. Thus the divisions below the months/moons varied greatly from weeks lasting five, seven and ten days to thirteen and even twenty days.[13] Hours could be decimal or sexagesimal. The traditional calendar system of India had subdivisions in the 24-hour system, equivalent to clock time units of 48 and 24 minutes, 48 and 24 seconds, right down to fractions of seconds. On the other end of the temporal scale, it operated with huge amounts of astronomical time that related to the life of Brahmā: one hour in the life of Brahmā equals 8.76 million human years.[14] Clearly, differences cannot be reduced to social development and functional need alone. Cosmology and religious factors played a central role, as did changes in political power, demographical issues – ancient Babylon, for example, was a city of some 250,000 inhabitants – and divergence in geography and climate conditions. Thus, for example, the sun played a much smaller role in Nordic countries, where it disappears for long periods during the dark winter months. For ancient Egyptians, in contrast, the annual flooding of the Nile together with the reappearance of Sirius in the night sky constituted the beginning of the year, while the gods Osiris, Isis and Horus were in charge of the three seasons associated with flooding, sowing and harvesting respectively.

From the above we can see that time reckoning in the form of calendar systems not only transcended the yearly cycle but also rendered problematic any neat separation into sacred and profane time. Furthermore, the notion of ancient life restricted to the seasonal round is clearly not sustainable as soon as we look carefully at what is entailed in the reckoning of time. The year becomes just one small unit in the wider scheme of cosmic rhythms, divine intent, and the cultural efforts to name, count and number. To know and name that which transcends human being was to get closer to the divine, to achieve a measure of predictability over the unknown, and to gain a sense of power over that which functions outside human control.[15]

The history of time reckoning also suggests that new political systems tended to bring about changes in the appropriation of time: 'new times' in the double meaning of the word. As David Landes explains with reference to China,

> The calendar was a prerequisite of sovereignty, like the right to mint coins. Knowledge of the right time and season was power, for it was this knowledge that governed both the acts of everyday life and decisions of state. Each emperor inaugurated his reign with the promulgation of this calendar, often different from the one that had preceded it. His court astronomers were the only persons who were permitted in principle to use time keeping and astronomical instruments or to engage in astronomical study. His time was China's time.[16]

In more recent history, France and Russia, during the eighteenth and twentieth centuries respectively, attempted to change the Gregorian calendar to suit their revolutionary political systems.[17] In both cases the failure shows on the one hand how a new system indeed requires new temporal organization, and on the other how both tradition and interdependence with other countries made nationally based calendar change impossible. The time had passed when individual countries could change their time reckoning system according to new national needs and ideological criteria. The stage had been set for the globalization of time, which depended on agreement by a significant number of countries across the globe. The successful efforts of Japan after the Meiji Restoration of 1868 to 'Westernise' its time system, in contrast, show that while changes towards national individualization failed, national changes based on the intention to integrate with and adapt to the wider norm were eminently successful.[18] Standardization and globalization rather than national individualism were to become the future direction of temporal organization.

Creating Clock Time

The failure of France and Russia to radically alter the calendar to suit their national requirements has to be appreciated in the context of changes in time reckoning associated with the smaller temporal units that had taken place across the world since the Middle Ages. The 24-hour day, divided into equal hours and further subdivisions, which existed alongside unequal hours (hours that vary in length depending on season), had been well established across the globe by the time France attempted its reform. This machine-based, rationalized 24-hour system measured a time whose subdivisions were based purely on convention, a time that operated independently of the variations that were the mark of planetary cycles. Precision rather than compromises of integration came to be the mark of a good clock. By the time the French sought to revolutionize the calendar, this other revolution in time reckoning was sufficiently advanced in its socioeconomic permeation to make that change seem superfluous and for it to be experienced as an inconvenience to be resisted.

The clock-time revolution, we need to appreciate, was a subtle one. It crept up on people, seduced them with the magic of a machine that kept time through night and fog, kept telling time come rain or shine. 'During the first seven centuries of the machine's existence,' wrote Lewis Mumford in his seminal essay on clock time, 'the categories of time and space underwent an extraordinary change and no aspect of life was left untouched by this transformation.'[19]

The clock, of course, was not the first instrument to measure units within the day–night (diurnal) cycle. Sundials and systems based on fire or the flow of water and sand had provided good service for the establishment of units within the diurnal cycle. They did, however, have their limitations: the sundial would not work during darkness and on cloudy days; water clocks had problems with freezing; sand and burning sticks required constant attention. Su Sung's water clock (clepsydra), produced in 1086 for the emperor of China, was, in Landes' words, 'one of the marvels of the age'.[20] Its movement replicated the cycles of the sun, moon and significant stars, as well as marking roughly the equivalent of a quarter-hour of clock time, that is, 14 minutes and 24 seconds of clock time, to be precise. The structure, which was water driven, was enormous and occupied a tower some forty feet high. It was adaptable to seasonal variation and capable of measuring unequal hours, so that it was eminently suited to the temporal regime of ancient Chinese society. The difficulty was not accuracy or adaptability but weather conditions, that is, freezing up during the cold periods of the year. The size of the clock meant that it was difficult to keep the water at temperatures above freezing throughout the year.

Islamic cultures experienced fewer of these climatic difficulties of freezing and cloud cover. Thus the combination of water clocks and sundials served them well. It enabled them to mark and track time with an astounding accuracy that far surpassed any of the early mechanical clocks of medieval Europe. Moreover, these non-mechanical devices measured time by means that appeared appropriate to the smooth and unidirectional flow of the phenomenon they measured. The mechanical clock, in contrast, worked on a counterintuitive principle: it tracked and represented the continuity through discontinuous oscillation. And yet, despite the lack of accuracy and counterintuitive function, the mechanical clock captured the medieval imagination, infused understanding and changed public and private social relations. In addition to independence from context, the clock technology had the potential to be developed in entirely new directions: it allowed for miniaturization, portability and personal/private use. As such it facilitated a change, detailed in E. P. Thompson's seminal paper 'Time, Work-Discipline and Industrial Capitalism' (1967), from obedience to the public call of time from the bell tower to internalized time discipline. Let us therefore look in a bit more detail at this clock time, see what it does and what kind of time it produces, before we consider what the impact might be on social relations.

The clock, we can state quite categorically, changed the meaning of time. The machine time supplanted (but never eradicated) the experiential understanding of time as change – as growth and ageing, seasonal variation, the difference between the past and future – and shifted the experience and meaning of time towards invariability, quantity and precise motion expressed by number. With the mechanical clock, time became dissociated from planetary rhythms and seasons, from change and ageing, from experience and memory. It became independent from time and space, self-sufficient, empty of meaning and thus apparently neutral. This allowed for entirely new associations, linkages and contents to be developed and imposed. As an invariable measure of length, time was amenable to mathematical use, infinite division and precise calculation. As a quantity it became not only an essential parameter in scientific investigation but also an economic resource that could be allocated, spent or saved. As abstract value it could be exchanged with other abstract values such as money. As money it entered economic calculations, became an item in banking and book-keeping, entered as opportunity cost and came to be tied to speed, efficiency and profit creation. As machine time it became naturalized as time *per se*, it became, in Mumford's words, 'the new medium of existence'.[21] Although the shift to clock-time relations occurred slowly over a period of some four hundred years,[22] the radical nature of the change cannot be overestimated: the machine time seeped deeply into the fabric of social life and spread like a spider's web across the globe, leaving those who resisted the new time defined as backward and old-fashioned.

What was it then that made the technologically most sophisticated cultures stay with technologies that measured uneven hours and had climatic limitations while the then relative backwater of central Europe went ahead with the development of a new technology that fundamentally altered temporal knowledge and relations? The historian David Landes locates the reasons for the differences in sociopolitical tradition and religious practice.[23] For China, the middle kingdom, the centre of the earth and the universe, a country that had always been at the forefront of technological development, the European clock time was (a) lacking accuracy, (b) inappropriate to a society organized to variable hours, and thus no more than an interesting toy, and (c) an affront to the emperor's self-esteem. For other societies differences in religious practices may explain the uneven uptake of the new technology. Thus Landes points to a number of distinct patterns in prayer practices. Both Jewish and Islamic religious codes, for example, stipulated the number of times prayers had to be conducted within the daily and annual cycle but did not specify an exact hour. Christians, in contrast, were directed to prayer at set times of, for example, the third, sixth and ninth hour. Ever since the sixth century AD, the canonical hours of Christianity have played an important role. This was especially the case in monasteries, from whence they came to be adopted and adapted for daily life. Max Weber's analysis of the monasteries' role in the changing relations of time during the Middle Ages in Europe,[24] which is outlined in chapter 2, is supported and enhanced by a number of historical and sociological investigations.[25] 'Setting the prayer time by the clock', Landes suggests, 'was no small matter. It represents the first step towards a liturgy independent of the natural cycle.'[26] As such it required different measuring instruments from prayer regimes that were structured to planetary cycles with their inherent seasonal and diurnal variations.

The machine time of the clock is a time cut loose from the temporality of body, nature and the cosmos, from context-bound being and spiritual existence. As such it eminently suited the ethos and fervour of the Protestant quest for salvation, which required strict ascetic regimes that transcended the needs and pleasures of the body. It seems no accident, therefore, that the majority of clockmakers were Protestants.[27] Dissociated from their religious roots, today's clock-time relations are largely oriented to a decontextualized economy and the disembodied rationality of science. As Mumford puts it, 'Time-keeping passed into time-serving and time-accounting into time-rationing. As this took place, Eternity ceased gradually to serve as measure and focus of human actions.'[28]

As it is melded and worked into our social relations, decontextualized and disembodied, clock time facilitates an acute present-orientation and a sense of distance, disconnection, independence even from the physical world and external influences. When a machine time, which has no consequences, no cause and effect, no accumulation, no irreversible change, no memory and no purpose, is employed as a synchronizing and organizational tool, an illusionary set of temporal relations are set in motion that become real in their lived consequences. In factories, people synchronized to the clock-time rhythm come to be treated as appendages to the machine. The machine time gets elevated as the norm to which they are expected to perform. Children are educated in accordance with its mechanistic beat. Public life is regulated to its invariable rhythm. Accuracy and precision, punctuality and the regularity of the clockwork become the socially valued ideals of conduct. With equalized and neutralized temporal relations, the breadth of social relations has been opened up to invisible control. The times of night and day, summer and winter, the northern and southern hemisphere become interchangeable. Times of youth and old age, gender and disability, of well-being, illness and stress are commutable under the rule of clock time. All times are equal under the clock. Time created to human design thus irrevocably changed the human–time relation. The ultimate transcendent and recalcitrant became malleable and manageable. It yielded to human control. With its aid, moreover, unprecedented rationalization and undreamed of levels of efficiency in productivity and social organization were to be achieved.

What is most important to note, however, is that the machine time has not replaced the temporality of the body, the earth and the cosmos. The diurnal cycle is unchanged by it. Seasons continue to mark the annual round. We still need to sleep – preferably at night – eat at certain intervals, and we continue to age and die. Despite the empty, neutral hours imposed as norm on public life, our experience of time is seething with differences. This is so obvious that there is no need to remind you of this with a long list of examples. The challenge is how to theorize the temporal discontinuity wrought by the social relations of clock time in the context of embodied continuity, how to conceptualize the past in the present, difference in relation to similarity. We will consider those questions at the end of this chapter. First, however, there are two more changes in time know-how to be outlined.

Mobilizing World Time

Empty, neutral and detemporalized, clock time is applicable anywhere, any time. As such, it provides an ideal base not just for standardization but also for export of this time across the globe. The railways were the first industry to standardize their time across long distances. In Britain, for example, this involved only a twenty minutes difference between London and Bristol, while in North America it entailed some fifty-plus local times on journeys from the east to west coast. In Britain and the US these changes were afoot from the middle of the eighteenth century. During earlier periods, keeping a unified, common time was not an issue due to the slowness of the transport. That is to say, when it took one day to travel thirty miles, the time difference between locations was not substantial compared with the travelling speed of today's trains or aeroplanes where, on a transcontinental flight, for example, we might traverse nine time zones in the same period.

In 1884 the International Meridian Conference met in Washington DC and delegates from twenty-five countries agreed to standardize time across the globe. This involved time zones being established every 15 degrees of longitude. Time and longitude are connected because the earth rotates around its axis 360 degrees over twenty-four hours, one hour being the equivalent of 15 degrees longitude. Longitude and (clock) time therefore can be expressed in terms of the other's measure: time in degrees and longitude in hours, minutes and seconds. Greenwich was designated the 0 meridian, with longitude one hour apart in each direction up to 180 degrees. In 1880 Britain had adopted Greenwich Mean Time (GMT) as the single legal time standard, and one year before the Meridian Conference, North America had instituted Standard Railway Time.[29] Today the system is naturalized to such an extent that we take for granted the need to reset watches as we travel across time zones and adjust the date as we cross the date line on a flight from the US to Australia. Travelling among the Aleutian Islands we can move back and forth over the date line, celebrating Christmas twice or avoiding it altogether.

For shipping, the quest to establish longitude was a battle for control. Ships needed to know longitude in order to navigate with safety.[30] The country that first solved the longitude problem was considered to have a tremendous headstart in control over the seas. The importance of the issue can be gleaned from the fact that from the late sixteenth century onwards huge rewards were promised to whoever found a viable solution. In 1714 an Act of Queen Anne, the 'Longitude Act', decreed the biggest prize money ever offered for an invention

> 'for such person or persons as shall discover longitude': £10,000 for any method capable of determining the ship's longitude to within one degree; £15,000 if determined within two-thirds of a degree, and £20,000 if determined within one half degree, or in other words, thirty nautical miles.[31]

It was John Harrison, a maker of long-case clocks, who finally succeeded in the task, producing a marine clock that was tested on two trials to the West Indies in 1761 and 1764. As the novelist Dava Sobel shows so persuasively in *Longitude*, even though Harrison's marine time-keeper performed better than required, getting the just reward proved almost more difficult than the invention of this prized object. Only when King George III intervened after Harrison built the fifth successful chronometer did Parliament finally agree to pay a substantial amount of the prize money.

Parallel work had been going on in France. While Harrison's work proved that you can build a clock that can keep accurate time at sea, Pierre Le Roy's invention, which was completed in 1766, laid the foundation for today's modern marine chronometers. Le Roy was never awarded anything for his invention. By 1800 the basic design was so sophisticated and production on a large scale so advanced that the design survived largely unaltered until quartz crystal technology revolutionized the entire field of time-keeping. The mobilization of standard time thus needs to be seen in the wider historical context of shipping and the enhanced globalization of trade this development in time reckoning facilitated.

The globalization of clock time was completed when, at 10.00 am on 1 July 1913, the Eiffel Tower transmitted the first time signal across the globe. Wireless signals travelling at the speed of light displaced local times and established one time for all: 1913 is the beginning of world time. Standard time and world time were the essential material condition for the global network of communication in both information and transport. They underpin the planning and organization of transnational businesses and global organizations, of national governments and local media companies, of airlines and financial traders. The values that come as a package attached to the social relations of clock time cover the globe where they work their imperialism silently, unaided and implacably.

Networking Instantaneity

Towards the end of the nineteenth century developments in technology once more fundamentally altered temporal relations. Not abstraction and decontextualization, however, but speed was the defining temporal feature of the communications revolution of the late nineteenth century. The historian Stephen Kern details its progression and locates it firmly in the cultural context.[32] He understands the innovations associated with acceleration as the material foundation for the conceptual reorientation that accompanied the changing experiences of time and space. Two innovations in particular are of interest to us here – the wireless telegraph and the telephone. Both facilitated instantaneity and simultaneity, which means the elimination of duration and succession. Both rendered space irrelevant for the transmission of information.

According to Kern the telegraph's development can be traced to James Clark Maxwell's theory of electromagnetic waves, which he put forward in 1864.[33] Thirteen years later those theoretical entities were produced in the laboratory and seven years after that Guglielmo Marconi found a practical application for them. He established the first coastal wireless station for communication with ships at sea. Again it was shipping, its safety and the potential for power and control, which was at the forefront of the new technology. In 1903 an international congress regulated the use of wireless telegraphy and by 1904 the Marconi Company had set up the first wireless news service with transmissions from Cornwall and Cape Cod. From then on, wireless signals criss-crossed the earth, connecting land stations with ships at sea, reporting on disasters from across the globe, often saving the lives of passengers and crew who previously would have sunk without trace together with their vessels.

With the capacity to partake in distant events as they are happening, the global present came into being. Irrespective of whether it is facilitated by the wireless telegraph, the telephone, satellite television or networked computers, this electronic present bestows on us powers that had previously been the preserve of gods. It makes us 'all-seeing', and endows us with the supernatural capacity of extraterrestrials to be everywhere at once and nowhere in particular. The physical constraints of bodies in space are transcended. Movement across space is dematerialized. This means space has been not merely rearranged but rendered irrelevant and time has been reconstituted: instantaneity and simultaneity have replaced sequence and duration. Tempo, timing and the relentless pursuit of acceleration cease to be an issue when information can be transmitted at the speed of light and received simultaneously at any node within the global system. Or so it seems.

In daily practice, of course, nothing is replaced; it is merely overshadowed or altered by the imposition of the new. First, bodies still move through space at the pace set by physical ability and technological aid. The discrepancy in speed of motion between bodies and physical objects on the one hand and electronic transmission of information on the other brought with it entirely new problems about synchronization and sequencing, new expectations of speed and nightmares of congestion and overload. It spawned logistics, a new branch of business. Second, with the upper limit of speed reached, acceleration ceases to be a panacea for competition. The competitive edge has to be wrought from entirely new vistas. Third, in the long and distinguished history of time control, the networked instantaneity raised the spectre of total loss of control. We will return to these important contemporary issues at various points during the last chapter.

When we now look back over the path we have taken thus far in the course of these five chapters we can recognize that tempering and transcendence are primarily responses to finitude and transience: tempering as the adaptation of the spirit to the inevitability of death, transience as the attempt to create individual immortality by alternative means. Time tracking and transformation, in contrast, are social answers to the rhythms and uncertainties of the cosmos, the living world and the body. Tracking and naming the changes impose order. Counting and numbering the repetitions create predictability, make daily life manageable. Transformation alters time. Through the creation of time to human design, rhythmicity is modified; certainty comes within reach; the control of time becomes an ever more pressing socioeconomic goal. *In the encounter with death and temporality the four responses of tempering, transcending, tracking and transforming are born.* The battle with time has continued; only the form it takes has changed and is still changing with context, need and technological aid.

Before-and-after, them-and-us become meaningless distinctions when we gather up the past in the present, see it as fundamentally implicated in our now. Dualistic categorizations lose their pertinence. Analyses that focus on the interdependence and unity of time tempering, transcendence, tracking and transformation construct ancient predecessors and spatially distant others as kindreds in effort and endeavour. They thus avoid the hierarchy of development that necessarily and ineluctably positions the contemporary as an advance on what went before. They acknowledge the accumulation, refinement and intensification of effort but show the taken-for-granted language of progress to be unjustifiable. Mead and the theorists of relative time, outlined in chapter 3, provide the insights that underpin and frame an inquiry of this kind, while the theorists of objective time, detailed in chapter 2, guide the more empirical aspects of the investigation.

INTERLUDE

TIME COMPLEXITIES & HIERARCHIES

Complex
Times Now:
Multiplicity lived
Present enfolding past
Planning with uncertainty
Control with indeterminacy
Futures implicated in the present
Rituals combined with chronologies
Communal times in contexts of difference
Transcendence in situations of embodied time
Time as gift in conditions of economic exchange
Speed is linked to productivity but quality takes time
Standardized industrial time superimposed on local times
Commodified time permeates the fabric of everyday existence

Temporal
Hierarchies:
Trade over giving
Commodity over caring
Speed over slow processes
Public time over private times
Financial wealth over time wealth
Clock time monopolizes vernacular times
Control of the future is valued over precaution
Industrial time is naturalized as norm worldwide
Deviance from the norm means sanctions & low status
Economic time is objective, lived times seen as subjective
Time created to industrial design is tool to create inferior others
Fast means profitable efficiency, slow inefficiency and backwardness

6
The Quest for Time Control

Since the beginning of life and human existence, time, space and matter have formed an inseparable unity. Since prehistory, as I have shown in previous chapters, societies have embodied the temporal relations of their members and institutions, past and present. This is so because all cultures, ancient and modern, have established collective ways of relating to the past and future, of synchronizing their activities, of coming to terms with finitude. *How* we extend ourselves into the past and future, *how* we pursue immortality and *how* we temporally manage, organize and regulate our social affairs, however, has been culturally, historically and contextually distinct. Each historical epoch with its new forms of socioeconomic expression is simultaneously restructuring its social relations of time. The industrial mode of life is no exception. To understand the temporal relations of industrial and industrializing societies requires us to grasp a number of interrelated approaches in their contextual continuity and discontinuity with other forms of temporal knowledge and social relations.

In the preceding chapters I have argued that the search for transcendence is primarily concerned with the finitude of earthly existence, and the pursuit of know-how with the rhythmicity of our environment. In this chapter I want to propose that the quest for control is to a large extent about obtaining dominion over time for economic gain and social advantage. For this to happen, the locus of control had to be transferred from natural and supernatural to human powers. It required secondly that the sin of usury had to be overcome: the forbidden practice converted into a Christian duty on the path to salvation. This transformation proceeded slowly between the early and late Middle Ages and, according to Max Weber, whose approach has been detailed in chapter 3, the Reformation had a major role to play in the metamorphosis of time from God's gift to *commodified, compressed, colonized* and *controlled* resource. These four Cs of industrial time – commodification, compression, colonization and control – will be the focus in these pages, the fifth C of the creation of clock time having been discussed already in the previous chapter. I show their interdependence and identify some of the socio-environmental impacts of those particular temporal relations.[1]

The creation of time to human design in an atemporal, decontextualized form, as outlined in chapter 5, was a necessary techno-material condition for the use of time by industrial societies as an abstract exchange value and for the acceleration, control and global imposition of time. Clock time, the human creation, as I have shown, operates according to fundamentally different principles from the ones underpinning the times of the cosmos, nature and the spiritual realm of eternity. It is a decontextualized empty time that ties the measurement of motion to expression by number. Not change, creativity and process, but static states are given a number value in the temporal frames of calendars and clocks. The artifice rather than the processes of cosmos, nature and spirit, we need to appreciate, came to be the object of trade, control and colonization.

Commodification

Much of contemporary social science writing on the commodification of time has its roots in Karl Marx's work on the subject matter in the *Grundrisse* and *Capital, Volume 1*. Thus, for example, Anthony Giddens draws on it extensively in his *A Contemporary Critique of Historical Materialism*

(1981). For David Harvey it forms the base to his analysis of the contemporary temporal relations under *The Condition of Postmodernity* (1989). I have outlined some of Marx's work on the subject towards the end of chapter 2 and will not repeat it here other than to remind you that Marx's principal point regarding the commodification of time was that an empty, abstract, quantifiable time that was applicable anywhere, any time was a precondition for its use as an abstract exchange value on the one hand and for the commodification of labour and nature on the other. Only on the basis of this neutral measure could time take such a pivotal position in all economic exchange.

When Marx's insights are conjoined to those of Max Weber, who traced the associated instrumental rationalization of time to a move from monastic practice to the Protestants' quest for salvation and the subsequent 'iron cage' of purely economic rational conduct,[2] we get a sense of the powerful forces at play. Today the time-is-money assumption permeates every aspect of daily life as naturalized and unquestioned fact. We talk of saving, spending or squandering time without giving much thought to what this might mean. As long as the commodification of time functions as a taken-for-granted feature of our lives the associated inequities remain invisible. The task for social theory, therefore, is to render the invisible visible, show relations and interconnections, begin the process of questioning the unquestioned. Before we can identify some of these economic relations of temporal inequity, however, we first need to understand in what way the sin of usury was a barrier to the development of economic life as we know it today in industrial societies.

From a Christian perspective, the selling of time for profit was a sin because time belonged not to human beings but God.[3] The trade in time was theft because it was trade in something that could not belong to individuals. As long as earnings on time were deemed to be a sin, the historian Jacques Le Goff explains, capitalism and the money economy could not develop, since, for the merchant, time was one of the prime opportunities for profit.[4] There could be no charging for interest, no trade in time, no utilization of time as abstract exchange value:

> The merchant's activity is based on assumptions of which time is the very foundation – storage in anticipation of famine, purchase for resale when the time is ripe, as determined by knowledge of economic conjunctures and the constants of the market in commodities and money – knowledge that implies the existence of an information network and the employment of couriers. Against the merchant's time the church sets up its own time, which is supposed to belong to god alone and which cannot be an object of lucre.[5]

In medieval Europe the Church as God's representative on earth was the keeper and guardian of time. Not even the sovereign had jurisdiction over it. The sovereign had the monopoly over weights and measures; the churches were in charge of time in all its forms, but most especially calendar time.

While interest and credit had been known and documented since 3000 BC in Babylonia, it was not until the late Middle Ages that the Christian Church slowly and almost surreptitiously changed its position on usury,[6] which set time free for trade, to be allocated, sold and controlled. It is against this background that we have to read the extracts from Benjamin Franklin's text of 1736, quoted at length in chapter 2, which contains the famous phrases 'Remember, that *time* is money . . . Remember that money begets money.'[7] Clock time, the created time to human design, was a precondition for this change in value and practice and formed the perfect partner to abstract, decontextualized money.

From the Middle Ages, trade fairs existed where the trade in time became commonplace and calculations about future prices an integral part of commerce. In addition, international trade by sea required complex calculations about potential profit and loss over long periods, given that trade ships might be away for as long as three years at a time. The time economy of interest and credit, moreover, fed directly into the monetary value of labour time, that is, paid employment as an integral part of the production of goods and services. However, it was not until the French Revolution that the individual (meaning male) ownership of time became enshrined as a legal right.[8]

When 'time is money' then time costs money and time makes money because the economic practice of charging interest means that capital has a built-in clock that is constantly ticking away. Every second, minute and hour, every day, month and year brings profit on the invested sum of money. Equally, every day, month and year that money is borrowed has to be paid for in interest. This inevitably leads to careful time calculations with respect to the costs arising from the time that goods are stored, that materials spend in warehouses before they are used in the production process, that goods spend in transit, that machines are running, and that products lie idle on the shelves before they are sold. Today the idea that time is money is so deeply entrenched in the industrial way of life that no aspect of social existence is exempt from its practical expression. It is implicated when mothers rush to get the children dressed for school, when we opt for the fastest mode of transport, when we are obliged to wait in the doctor's surgery.

Closer inspection makes it apparent that the unifying clock-time economy of money divides as it unites: not everyone's time is of equal value. While the money rich tend to be time poor, they can exchange their money for time. They can buy labour-saving devices and they can purchase the time of others in the form of skills and services to make up the shortfall of their own time. For the time rich and money poor, in contrast, the equivalent exchange tends not to be an option. The time of children and the elderly, of (unremunerated/ unemployed) single parents and carers, of subsistence farmers (predominantly women) and those locked into bartering relations tends not to provide them with a basis for economic wealth creation. As 'unproductive' labour, their unremunerated work in household and school, care relations and food production is rendered invisible, their time decreed 'worthless'. Outside the charmed circle of the tightly delimited time economy, their time gets positioned at the bottom of the hierarchy of temporal relations.

Since the impact of social relations organized to empty, neutral clock time is anything but unbiased in its effects, we need to ask whose time is valuable to whom and whether or not the value involved can and should be translated into money. This means that social science analyses need to go beyond the decontextualized economic investigation of institutions and encompass some of the context-dependent effects on people's everyday lives. They need to understand as inseparable the relations of time and their socio-environmental impacts, underlying assumptions and their material expressions, institutional processes and recipients' experiences, hidden agendas and power relations, unquestioned time politics and 'othering' practices.[9] The temptation to focus exclusively on the economy or technology, on science or the mode of information, therefore needs to be resisted, simplicity foregone in favour of the disconcerting messiness of complexity in motion.

Compressions

In *Time Wars* Jeremy Rifkin identifies the centrality of speed valorization for the industrial way of life.

> If centralization, concentration, and accumulation epitomized the bigger-is-better theme of spatial politics, then efficiency and speed characterize the time values of the modern age . . . The Idea of saving and compressing time has been stamped into the psyche of Western civilization and now much of the world.[10]

Where (clock) time is equated with money, speed becomes an important economic value, since the faster a product can be produced, the less money-time is tied up in the process in the form of machinery, interest payments and labour costs. The faster the product can be moved through the system from production to consumption the higher is the profit potential. An alternative way of expressing speed is time compression, the preferred term of Karl Marx and more recently David Harvey.[11]

In economic production, time compression has been achieved by a number of means: by increasing the activity within the same unit of time (through machines and the intensification of labour), reorganizing the sequence and ordering of activities (Taylorism and Fordism), using peaks and troughs more effectively (flexibilization), and by eliminating all unproductive times from the process (the just-in-time system of production, delivery and consumption). Time compression is an unquestioned economic and political goal as it increases profit and shows up positively in a country's gross national product (GNP).

At the same time, we need to appreciate that speed valorization is not exclusively a phenomenon of modernity. Speed of movement and reaction, for example, is associated with competitive advantage across species and in many cases vital to survival. Moreover, much of the history of technology can be read as advances in speed, the different wheel and vehicle technologies and various modes of production being key examples. Seen from this perspective, contemporary acceleration and speed valorization are mere variants on the ancient theme of cultural engagement with the time-space limits set by nature. And yet, despite the continuities, there are discontinuities that are worthy of our attention.

The cultural historian Stephen Kern details some of the changes that took place at the turn of the last century. He shows how, during the period from 1880 to 1919, innovations in technology, art, literature and science mutually influenced and inspired each other.[12] The achievement of higher speeds was integral to those developments and permeated the very structure of society. It inspired artists and architects, novelists and poets, whose avant-garde work in turn fired the imagination of scientists and engineers. Motorized transport (trains, cars, aeroplanes) and machine-based production, electricity and gas, film and electronic communication (telegraph, wireless and telephone), are all developments associated with that period, which changed the way people viewed, understood and related to their world.

In the midst of this explosion in speed anything seemed possible. In 1895 H. G. Wells published *The Time Machine* in which he postulated time travel. In 1909 the artist and poet Filippo Tommaso Marinetti founded the Futurist movement, which sought to create entirely new and bold futures. Through a series of manifestos Marinetti made public the Futurists' frequently outrageous claims.

> Why should we look back when what we want is to break down the mysterious doors of the impossible? Time and space died yesterday. We already live in the absolute, because we have created eternal, omnipresent speed.[13]

> The world's magnificence has been enriched by a new beauty; the beauty of speed . . . We cooperate with mechanics on destroying the old poetry of distance and wild solitudes, the exquisite nostalgia of parting for which we substitute the tragic lyricism of ubiquity and omnipresent speed.[14]

The speed that is celebrated here was in no way tied to the time economy of money. That would have seemed an abhorrently bourgeois idea to its proponents. And yet we need to ask whether or not the abstraction of speed, the celebration of acceleration and the control of the future would have been possible without the prior transformation of time into clock time and whether or not such valorization makes sense without the underpinning deep structure of the time economy of money.

The French political theorist and technology critic Paul Virilio has studied the history of technological development not just over that crucial period at the turn from the nineteenth into the twentieth century but over the last two hundred years.[15] Virilio suggests that we can read the history of modernity as a series of innovations in ever-increasing time compression. He argues that, through the ages, the wealth and power associated with ownership of land was equally tied to the capacity to traverse it and to the speed at which this could be achieved. He likened this speed-based wealth to military prowess, which is inescapably tied to the speed of movement by bodies and missiles across space. He focused his analysis on speed around three Ts of increasing tempo. These encompass nineteenth-century *transport*, twentieth-century *transmission* and twenty-first century *transplantation*, each with their own distinct means of enhancing independence of the social relations of time from space and the body.

With nineteenth-century transport the relation of time and space has been altered. The invention of trains, cars and aeroplanes at the turn of the last century massively increased the speed with which bodies could move across space and dramatically shortened the time involved.[16] Since their inception, all improvements in these modes of transport have been primarily in time compression. Virilio shows how the dramatic advances in speed were accompanied by a number of contradictions and paradoxes. Thus, for example, while cars, planes and trains had become progressively faster, the time spent in transit had not been compressed at an equal rate. Standstill and traffic jams, snails' pace and stop-go progression are key features of today's traffic around urban centres. Endless queues in crowded lobbies are a mark of travel by plane, delays and cancellations an integral part of commuting by train. In the light of this evidence, which is fully supported by transport research,[17] Virilio formulated the *dromological* law, which states that increase in speed increases the potential for gridlock.[18]

A second inconsistency in the acceleration associated with transport relates to the speed-energy-pollution constellation where, as Rifkin and Howard point out, 'the faster we speed up, the faster we degrade.'[19] Virilio writes despairingly about the social sciences' failure to see and theorize these environmental connections. A third paradox is only hinted at by Virilio, when he suggests that conflict is to be expected between democracy and *dromocracy*, the politics that take account of time and the speed of movement across space.[20] It concerns the sociopolitical and socioeconomic relations associated with advances in transport speed, which affect different individuals, groups and classes of society in uneven ways. Thus, for example, the money-rich-time-poor can use their wealth to purchase speed, while the time-rich-money-poor cannot use their time to purchase wealth, that is, exchange their excess time for money. Equally, the traffic jams and waiting times affect different groups of society in unequal ways. Not only the technological developments associated with increased transport speeds, therefore, but also associated economic relations as well as the allied politics and policies thus need to feature centrally in the analysis.

With respect to twentieth-century transmission Virilio has in mind the wireless telegraph, telephone, radio and subsequent developments in computer and satellite communication, which have once more changed the relationship between time and movement across space. Together, these innovations in transmission replaced succession and duration with seeming simultaneity and instantaneity. Duration has been compressed to zero and the present extended spatially to encircle the globe: it became a global present. Globally accessible events and the possibility of concerted action in 'real time' bring into one frame of reference causal and non-causal, instantaneous and sequential processes. The intensive (electronic) present, Virilio suggests, is no longer part of chronological time; we have to conceptualize it instead as *chronoscopic* time. Real space, he argues, is making room for decontextualized 'real-time' processes and intensity takes over from extensity.[21] This in turn has consequences and, similar to the time compression in transport, the compression in transmission has led to a range of paradoxical effects.

> The teletechnologies of real time are . . . killing 'present' time by isolating it from its here and now, in favour of a communicative elsewhere that no longer has anything to do with our 'concrete present' in the world, but is the elsewhere of a 'discreet telepresence' that remains a complete mystery.[22]

Here too we find contradictions and paradoxes. The overload of information, for example, is becoming so extensive that taking advantage of only the tiniest fraction of it not only blows apart the principle of instantaneity and 'real-time' communication, but also slows down operators to a point where they lose themselves in the eternity of electronically networked information. Secondly, the potential capacity of exterritorial beings to be everywhere at once and nowhere in particular is inescapably tied to operators that are bounded by their embodied temporal limits of terrestrial existence and sequential information processing. The actual capacity for parallel absorption of knowledge, therefore, is hugely disappointing. Equally, the electronic capacity to be now-here and no-where has brought the body to a standstill. 'We have finally achieved states', Virilio suggests, that border 'on sensory deprivation'.[23] Elsewhere he calls it 'growing inertia'.[24] In this area of electronic speed intensification, I am afraid, Virilio's pertinent technology critique does not reach deep enough into the social fabric where the compressions are worked into entirely new structures and social relations of inequity.

Zygmunt Bauman's analysis, for example, points to the exterritorial nature of power when he suggests that, for capitalist relations, communication at the speed of light means freedom from space.[25] When business has attained such liberation from locality it is freed from responsibility and obligation to that local/national community. It can relocate to wherever and whenever profit beckons and abandon those bound to their locality to deal with the consequences: to bear the cost of the social and environmental devastation, the regeneration programmes, the depopulation of rural communities. Baumann suggests further that those at the receiving end of the space-transcending, time-compressing information revolution are confronted with the time equivalent of earlier spatial enclosures. In the case of electronic enclosures, people are barred from access to the high-speed world of information despite ostensibly open access. Money, skill and life chances more generally turn out to be highly effective barriers to this speeded-up world of knowledge production and information overload.

Virilio identifies the time compression afforded by twenty-first century transplantation primarily with prostheses provided by xenotransplantation and nanotechnology. In an essay entitled 'From Superman to Hyperactive Man', Virilio suggests:

> After yesterday's *superstructure* and *infrastructure*, we might now envisage a third term, *intrastructure*, since the very recent advent of nanotechnological miniaturization promotes biotechnology's physiological intrusion into, or insemination of, the living organism.[26]

Time-compressing technological innovation, he argues, has moved from the vastness of planetary and earthly space to the micro spaces of organs and cells to what he calls *'the heart of the living'*.[27] In writing that is part reportage, part postulation he sees artificial rhythms replace natural ones: to be speeded up at will and paced to the dictates of the prosthetic machine.

> For the biologist, *excitability is the fundamental property of living tissue* . . . If it is to be excited, then to *be alive is to be speed*, a metabolic speed that technology is compelled to increase and improve, the way it has done with animal species.[28]

While much of Virilio's work on acceleration through transplantation is projective and speculative, we can see how genetic modification of plants and animals has already achieved a phenomenal increase in speed of change. With genotechnology scientists have the capacity to reduce to an instant what took generations to achieve with conventional breeding methods. It is not just that this particular intensification of processes holds out the promise of phenomenal economic rewards, it has equally enormous sociopolitical implications for control, accountability and responsibility, which we will revisit at later points in the chapter.

From the above we can see that Virilio understands human history in terms of a race with time, of ever-increasing speeds that transcend humans' biological capacity. To theorize culture without the dromosphere, that is, the sphere of beings in motion, he therefore suggests, misses the key point of cultural activity and the uniqueness of the industrial way of life. Without an explicit conceptualization of the contemporary dromosphere – or in my terms *timescape* – it is thus difficult to fully understand the human-technology-science-economy-equity-environment constellation. Moreover, it becomes impossible to appreciate that people are the weakest link when the time frames of action are compressed to zero and effects expand to eternity, when transmission and transplantation are instantaneous but their outcomes extend into an open future, when instantaneity and eternity are combined in a discordant fusion of all times. Virilio's work forcefully demonstrates that the political economy of wealth is not the sole motor of cultural change.

For an analysis that treats seriously the relation between technology and the political economy we have to turn to Manuel Castells's *The Rise of the Network Society* (1996). In this work the seductive elegance of Virilio's 3-T analysis gives way to a comprehensive, complex and detailed historical weaving together of technological, economic, political and social forces. Here, practices based on underlying assumptions are related to implicit technological principles, processes to products, intentions to unintended consequences. In Castells's analysis, time is not merely compressed but processed, and it is the network rather than acceleration that constitutes the discontinuity in a context of continuing compression.

In a systematic analysis Castells contrasts the clock time of modernity with the network time of the network society. He demonstrates the importance of time zones as sources of competitive advantage in capital markets that operate in a context of real-time communication. This network time transforms social time into two allied but distinct forms: simultaneity and timelessness.[29] Simultaneity refers to the globally networked immediacy of communication provided by satellite television and the internet, which makes real-time exchanges possible irrespective of the distances involved. Timelessness, the more problematic concept, refers to the layering of time, the mixing of tenses, the editing of sequences, the splicing together of unrelated events. It points to the general loss of chronological order and context-dependent rhythmicity. It combines eternity with ephemerality, real time with contextual change. Castells designates timeless time as 'the dominant temporality of our society', which occurs when

> the informational paradigm and the network society induce systematic perturbations in the sequential order of phenomena . . . This perturbation may take the form of compressing the occurrence of phenomena, aiming at instantaneity, or else by introducing random discontinuity in the sequence. Elimination of sequencing creates undifferentiated time, which is tantamount to eternity.[30]

Castells, like Virilio, resists an overly economized analysis without, however, losing sight of the complexity of socio-economic, political and environmental processes that have such a powerful role to play in the creation of modern culture, with its age and class as well as gender and culture-specific 'glocal' inequities.

> The eternal/ephemeral time of the new culture does fit with the logic of flexible capitalism and with the dynamics of the network society, but it adds its own, powerful layer, installing individual dreams and collective representations in a no-time mental landscape.[31]

This new culture is perceptively theorized by Robert Hassan, who suggests that emphasis on 'real time' misses the point. At issue are the network and the associated interconnectivity, not the speed of communication. 'Interconnectivity', Hassan suggests, 'is what gives the network time its power within culture and society.'[32] It is worth quoting him at length here.

> Network time does not 'kill' or render 'timeless' other temporalities, clock-time or otherwise. The embedded nature of the 'multiplicity' of temporalities that pervade culture and society, and the deeply intractable relationship we have with the clock make this unlikely. Rather, the process is one of 'displacement'. Network time constitutes a new and powerful temporality that is beginning to displace, neutralise, sublimate and otherwise upset other temporal relationships in our work, home and leisure environments.[33]

In an important move Hassan then links the revolution in information and communication technology to neoliberal globalization and to what Ulrich Beck calls 'organized irresponsibility'.[34] With this move Hassan takes the analysis into new directions and opens up a space for critical thought and action.

Colonization

Time has been a most effective colonizing tool. That which has become taken for granted is an ideal vehicle for imperialist purposes since it is no longer discussed and no longer visible. When standard time and world time were established at the beginning of the last century, this significant change engendered impassioned debate and resistance. When today the values associated with this artefactual, commodified time are imposed as norm on societies who organize their lives according to different temporal principles, attempts at discussion about its merits are greeted with incredulity. Furthermore, resistance is met with incomprehension since clock time and commodified time have become an unquestioned and inescapable fact of the industrial way of life. Any group or society that deviates from this 'norm' or endeavours to question its wisdom, value and desirability is considered backward, lazy, uncivilized.

There are two sides to the colonization of time: the global imposition of a particular kind of time which is colonization *with* time, and the social incursion *into* time – past and future, night-time and seasons, for example – which is the colonization *of* time. Colonization *with* time therefore refers to the export of clock and commodified time as unquestioned and unquestionable standard, colonization *of* time to the scientific, technological and economic reach into time – most usually of distant others who have no say in the matter.

Colonization *with* time has been achieved with the aid of standard time, time zones and world time, on the one hand, and with the globalization of industrial time and its associated economic values as common-sense norm, on the other. In the latter case it is the time values and the social relations of industrial time that are being *adopted* as well as *imposed* on a worldwide basis. As I indicated in the previous chapter, Japan and Russia proceeded to 'Westernize' their social relations of time, thus accepting the Western convention as norm and as a value to be embraced and emulated. The political leaders of both societies considered this to be a precondition for becoming a fully fledged industrial nation, which was equated with being 'modern', 'progressive', even 'civilized'. They also realized that there was a heavy economic and political price to pay for any deviance from the industrial norm. In most cases of third world 'development', however, clock time is imposed as norm irrespective of its suitability, and whether or not the recipients consider it desirable.[35]

This industrial norm, as I suggested above, is fundamentally rooted in clock time and underpinned by naturalized assumptions about not just the capacity but also the need to commodify, compress and control time. The elements of this package of industrial time are both cumulative and mutually supporting and form a coherent, integrated dis/continuous whole. As long as the underpinning assumptions remain naturalized, taken for granted and unquestioned, unwilling recipients will find it difficult if not impossible to make their protests heard and understood, let alone accepted as meaningful and legitimate. Only when fault lines in the logic become exposed and irresolvable contradictions begin to destroy the system from within can alternative visions take hold and openings for change be operationalized.

While the colonization *with* clock time is a relatively recent phenomenon, the colonization *of* time has an exceedingly long history. Night-time and the cold periods of the year, for example, have been colonized since at least the harnessing of fire. And yet, as Murray Melbin's and Stephen Kern's work shows,[36] some significant dis/continuities have emerged with industrialization and the technologies of the late nineteenth and early twentieth centuries. Publicly available gas and electricity, for example, have fundamentally altered our relation to the hours of darkness and the seasons. If, with the mere flicking of a switch, night can be turned into day, while summer and winter become interchangeable through heating and air-conditioning, then much of the skill and mystique has been taken out of these time-transcending practices. Dance, magic and ritual are no longer required to pacify the spirits that have been disturbed by the time-transcending intrusion. Today, the colonization of the night and seasons has become mundane, taken for granted, to be recognized in the enormity of its achievement only when it breaks down: when the supply of gas and electricity fails, when darkness, cold and heat remind us of the 'natural condition'.[37]

In a similar vein we could say that the colonization of past and future has been practised throughout human history, that the transcendence of the present, as I have argued previously, is a mark of culture. In the time-transcending practices I discussed in chapter 4, the efforts were focused on death and finitude, on transience and ephemerality, on seasons and planetary rhythms. Clearly, this is not the only way that industrial societies extend themselves into the future. What then characterizes industrial societies' colonization of time? What differentiates it from other forms of time transcendence? How does the continuity relate to the discontinuity?

In order for the dis/continuity to become apparent, the creation of time to human design, its commodification and compression and its (re)formulation in Newtonian science have to be seen together as mutually supporting and implicating features that construct time as an externalized object, abstracted from the change processes and the phenomena that constitute it.[38] The arrangement in the box offers another way of representing its clustered uniqueness and discontinuity with earlier time-transcending practices.[39] It demonstrates

political time	scientific time	economic time
use	**use**	**use**
regulate time	measure time	use as resource
define time values	create clock time	commodify time
impose time values	impose clock time on nature	impose economic time norm
control (and discount) future	control (and discount) future	control and discount future
globalize clock time	colonize all time	globalize time economy
time is:	**time is:**	**time is:**
clock time	clock time	clock time
decontextualized	decontextualized	decontextualized
quantified	quantified	quantified
linear	linear	linear
invariant	invariant	invariant
external	external	external

very clearly that clock time permeates the key institutions of industrial society. It shows that irrespective of the diverse temporal uses of time in the political, scientific and economic spheres, a unified clock time underpins the differences in expressions. All other forms of temporal relations are refracted through this created temporal form, or at least touched by its pervasive dominance.

Once time is disembedded, that is, extracted from process and product, it becomes an object and as such subject to bounding, exchange and transformation.[40] It is in this form that time is colonized, as distinct from the time embedded in events and processes, which has been subject to cultural efforts of transcendence. It is in the objectified form that the future features in economic activity and becomes the object of colonization for science. The *effects* of the economic and scientific colonizing practices, in contrast, are felt at the lived level of embedded time as intergenerational inequity, environmental disasters and cultural destruction.[41]

In economic theory time is a scarce resource. To augment the scarcity, economists seek to expand the resource through incursions into past and future. Economic theorists such as Gary Becker and Clifford Sharp argue that the scarcity of time derives from our finite existence, that it is the limited amount of time we have allotted to us during our lifetime, which makes time the principal resource in all economic activity.[42] The problem with this premise is that in order for us to think and talk about time in terms of a quantitative resource that can be used and allocated, it first had to be disembedded into a distinct entity. Thus we find no such talk or conception in cultures where time is embedded in events, phenomena and processes. Such cultures seek to transcend the *temporality of earthly existence* rather than colonize time *per se*. The difference may become clearer when we put side by side industrial societies' colonization of the past and the gathering up of the past of ritual practice. Both 'transport' the past into the present but they do it on the basis of fundamentally different principles and assumptions.[43]

In ritual and myth the past is gathered up in the present to connect origin to destiny, to fuse past practices and experiences with present ones in order to integrate all of existence into a living whole. We may describe this process as presencing or enpresencing. The past here is *not* conceived as an independent resource for exploitation and enhancement of knowledge or economic wealth, whereas this is precisely the basis on which we can talk about colonization of the past. Archaeology, astronomy and geology, for example, provide knowledge of the very distant past which may hold useful insights for the prediction of future developments. Entire industries are building up around the uncovering of the past, that is, the interpretation, representation and reconstruction of the past, both ancient and more recent, for extractive use in the present. Here the past is conceived as an independent resource available for exploitation in the present. This (economic) utilitarian perspective applies almost regardless of application. Distant planets and black holes, our earth history, the lives of ancient cultures, the consumption of heritage, all are resource pasts to be colonized. The basis of this time resource, however, is not the finitude of individual life but the objectification of time. Only as independent, objectified resource can the past be colonized and economically allocated, sold and controlled.

A similar relation pertains to the colonization of the future, which enables us once more to distinguish between transcendence, as outlined in chapter 4, and colonization. The future means uncertainty for present action. Accordingly, the issue of uncertainty is the second way economic theory engages with the issue of time.[44] Anthony Giddens addresses the colonization of the future as a social theorist when he suggests that 'modern capitalism embeds itself into the future by calculating future profit and loss, and thereby risk, as a continuous process.'[45] Capitalism is distinct in its relationship to the future whether this be in its systems of credit and interest, insurance or financial trading. Thus, for example, since the sixteenth century the insurance system has redistributed risk. It makes projections about the future on the basis of a known past and promises to financially compensate future loss in exchange for payments in the present. Whether this economic engagement with the future operates at the private, commercial or (welfare) state level, it is based on the belief that the future is amenable to human regulation, extractive exploitation and design in the present.

Furthermore, as I noted in the previous chapter, since the latter part of the Middle Ages the economic future has been understood with reference to the threats, costs and benefits it holds for the present. The economy therefore operates in the sphere between present and future with a view to using the future to secure the present. To achieve that task, it borrows from the future to finance the present. The radical present orientation is demonstrated at its fiercest in the discounting of the future, a convention that is deeply embedded across the breadth of economic theory and practice. Here the value of the future is calculated with reference to the use and extractive value it holds for the present. This applies for both the good and the bad. Thus, for example, an environmental problem such as radiation contamination for successor generations is rendered 'harmless' by the economic sleight of hand that calculates the potential problems with reference to what the contamination means for us in the present: the larger the temporal distance of radiation, the less cost it is to us – so, no problem.[46]

The scientific colonization of the future operates on very similar principles and assumptions. Like the economy, the work of science reaches into the future. This scientific future is projected and predicted, planned and programmed, pursued and pre-empted, procured and polluted. Knowledge of the past is the basis on which the future is known and forged, foretold and foreclosed, on which innovation is justified and safety established. This applies whether we refer to the chemical, nuclear or biotechnological future. The discounting attitude creeps into scientific reasoning with the what's-in-it-for-us-now approach, which might apply to one or all of the following: economic gain, academic prestige, job security, nationally based pride in scientific prowess.

Genetic manipulation of food crops can serve as example here. With the genetic modification of food, science has achieved a temporal equivalent of spatial globalization. It has extended the scientific reach to the beginning and end of time. The totality of time is invoked on the basis that modification of organisms with genetic material from other species means drawing on genetic bases that have been shared by all life forms since the beginning of the evolution of life, while the effects of those modified organisms in the environment are open to an indefinite, unbounded future: uncontrolled and uncontrollable. The potential for economic gain is enormous. The scientific, individual and national prestige involved is of such magnitude that, no matter how strongly public opinion is amassed against this scientific colonization of time, developments in the genetic modification of food continue unabated with the full support of national governments.

Such radical present-orientation, be this in economics, science or politics, makes parasitic use of the future – our own and that of successor generations. Helga Nowotny conceptualizes those incursions as 'extended present', as a future that is organized, regulated, tamed, safeguarded, colonized and foreclosed *now*.[47] This is a political act for which perpetrators are not and cannot be held accountable and the potentially affected do not and cannot get redress as long as the five Cs of industrial time – creation, commodification, compression, colonization and control – continue to be applied and imposed as the naturalized norm. Moreover, while the colonization of the future is accomplished on the basis of objectified time, its unintended (and intended?) consequences are played out in the lived temporalities of nature, the intricate choreography of rhythms, in successors' bodies and environments. The abstract and the lived become inseparable as soon as the conceptions get activated in practice and the materialized ideas are inserted in processes. Dis/continuity therefore is the challenge for a social theory of time, with bringing together what conventional analyses have set apart the task for the immediate social science future.

Control

When we now look at the breadth of responses to earthly time, we can see that social time cannot be encompassed by either the quest for speed and acceleration, or the allocation of time as a scarce resource. Tempering and transcendence, knowledge and know-how, creation and control, I want to argue, are the three pillars around which the various engagements with time have been formed and are still forming. Control is the overarching concept for the five Cs of time – creation, commodification, compression, colonization and control – that mark the distinctiveness of industrial societies' public temporal relations. This control cluster of the five Cs of time, I have suggested, needs to be differentiated from both time tempering and transcendence, on the one hand, and time knowledge and know-how, on the other, since only in the control cluster is time objectified, externalized and constructed to specific design principles.

What then are the 'bare bones', the base structure that we were dealing with when we were focusing on practices associated with time tempering and transcendence, knowledge and know-how, creation and control? I propose that we think about temporal relations with reference to a cluster of temporal features, each implicated in all the others but not necessarily of equal importance in each instance. We might call this cluster a *timescape*. The notion of 'scape' is important here as it indicates, first, that time is inseparable from space and matter, and second, that context matters. When we consider the dominant, public timescape of industrial temporal relations, each of the temporal features identified in the basic timescape cluster is associated with a number of particular practices of transcendence and transformation. In the box overleaf the two timescapes are schematically summarized.

The listed practices in the industrial timescape cluster should be taken as indicative rather than exhaustive and contextualized in the time politics of liberal democracy, science and the global economy.

Grouping practices around a number of time Ts and giving physical shape to the classifications makes their constructed and provisional nature visible. It entices us to embrace multiplicity and explicitly acknowledge the constructed nature of knowledge. At the same time we need to be aware that any system of classification is binding and bounding, is blinding us to processes. With classifications we create pockets of order, invariance and stability in the sea of change complexity. 'Classing remains a static act,' as Michel Serres points out, 'it is the most effective obstruction against strong flux, to disperse it between baffles, to slow it down, to stop it, to freeze it.'[48] Clearly, we cannot theorize and analyse without some form of classification, which inevitably means some form of

---

Timescape comprises:
Time frames: seconds, days, years, lifetimes, eras, epochs
Temporality: process, irreversibility, impermanence
Tempo: pace, intensity/rate of activity
Timing: synchronization, Kairos
Time point: moment, Now, instant, juncture
Time patterns: rhythmicity, periodicity, cyclicality
Time sequence: series, cause and effect/simultaneity
Time extensions: duration, continuity: instant to eternity
Time past, present, future: horizons, memory, anticipation
The time entailed is multiplex

Public industrial timescapes comprise:
Time frames: quantity measured, resource, commodity
Temporality: measured, fixed, regulated, controlled
Timing: rationalized, as cost to be externalized
Tempo: increased, maximized, optimized
Time point: extended, commodified
Time patterns: evened out
Time sequences: controlled and edited
Time extensions: investment, opportunity cost, goal
Time Future: prospected, produced, predicted, pre-empted
Multiplex dis/continuity accomplished in practice

freezing processes. What is important, therefore, is that we remain cognisant of the classing action and its effects, the imposition and the product, and that we avoid conflating the construction with the processes under consideration.

Looking at the schematic representation of the industrial timescape, the first thing to appreciate is that the control over the objectified resource leaves no temporal feature untouched. Time frames and timing, temporality and tempo, time point, duration and succession have all become subject to control, that is, to speeding up and slowing down, to rearrangement of sequence and order, to evening out and accentuating of peaks and troughs. The variable, rhythmic times of life are regulated and disciplined to conform to uniform, invariable temporal patterns. Through socioeconomic technologies, transport, transmission and transplantation, time is compressed and processed. Clock time is used to regulate and rationalize the pace and seasonality of organisms and beings, social activities and institutions. With its aid rhythmicity is transformed into a rationalized beat.

The principles at the root of the successes of time control, however, are also becoming the sources of its demise. Industrial food production can serve as a first example. The industrial way of producing food is well placed to illustrate both the complexity and the paradoxical results of time control. Its achievements include the speeding up of growth and maturation and the control of the rate of ripening and decay during production and transit, storage and shelf-life. Fallow periods have been transformed into productive ones. The dormant season is as much as possible negated or at least shortened by artificial means through, for example, electric light, hydroculture and/or genetic modification. As part of contemporary industrial societies' overall project of rationalization and predictable control, the control of time is extended to the seasonal rhythmicity of nature, to the variable patterns and cycles of activity and rest, growth and decay. Sexual, seasonal and maturational rhythms are hormonally regulated. Their genetic control is busily worked on in science laboratories across the world. This impressive level of time control, however, is almost invariably accompanied by an equivalent loss of control over (unintended) consequences. As Castells notes, the mastery of time and the control of rhythms restructure temporality and, in the process, usher in contra-dictory logics.[49] Thus efforts to impose an invariable beat on the variable rhythmicity of life, to speed up and slow down species-specific rates of growth and decay, and to extend or shorten processes of ripening and maturation, are under-mined by disease and crop failure, threats to public safety and consumer boycotts.

With the temporal innovations in transport, transmission and transplantation, we have seen already how the increase in mastery is accompanied by a decrease in control. Electronic transmission is a particularly strong case in point. Time has been compressed to its limit; space eliminated in the process. Information and money move at the speed of light. No-where and now-here have become interchangeable. This allows for trillions of dollars to circulate and change virtual hands every day. However, as Mark Poster points out, 'the new level of interconnectivity heightens the fragility of the social net-works.'[50] The source of control now undermines its execu-tion. For clock time to exist and thus to be measurable and controllable there has to be duration, an interval between two points in time. Without duration there is no before and after, no cause and effect, no stretch of time to be measured. The principles of instantaneity and simultaneity of action across space, as I have shown in chapter 3, are encountered in quantum physics; they have no place in the Newtonian world of causality and bodies in motion, the world that we as embodied beings inhabit. The control of time that has reached the limit of compression has been shifted into a time world where notions of control are meaningless. More like the realm of myths and mysticism, the electronic world of interchangeable no-where and now-here requires knowledge and modes of being that are alien to the industrial way of life. Other modes of temporal existence, therefore, may hold some vital keys, their 'primitive' understanding of time point-ing not to control but to more appropriate ways of being in the realm of instantaneity.

With the transplantation of genes, science controls not just nature's products but its processes. It controls time at the level of *re*production, which means it controls life and the temporal-ity of being. Genotechnology, therefore, has the potential of realizing the time rationalizers' dream: precise control of

*re*production and instantaneous change in unlimited quanti-
ties. Changes introduced in the present may alter the life
course and evolution forever. However, here too control
achieved in the laboratory is not matched by control over
environmental outcomes. Control is relinquished once the
gene has been spliced into the organism and once that modified reproductive organism has been released into the environment.[51] This is the context of reflexive modernization, to
use Ulrich Beck's term,[52] where the source of successes is
implicated in excesses and where the principles underpinning
the industrial system undermine it from within, destroy its
base of existence, thus confronting us with questions of
meaning.

At the end of the quest for control we have come full circle
to where we started the book. What has slipped out of sight
with the industrial way of life emerges from the shadow. We
are once more confronted with questions about collective life
and death, origin and destiny. Intuitively, some of the public
protestors against genetic modification (and nuclear power)
seem to have grasped the depth of the issues in question. Our
politicians have not. A significant number of scientists are
aware but pursuing powerful agendas that bracket those
unsettling ideas and concentrate instead on seeing their work
as part of the solution, that is, the route to a new and better
destiny. Modern science located individual immortality in the
genes; it embodied transcendence. By working on the gene
itself, contemporary science has (re)introduced collective
immortality, forging collective embodied futures to eternity.
The quest to *create* alternative futures has found its holy grail,
while, the quest for *control* is failing proportional to its
successes.

The pursuit of temporal control confronts us with the
(im)possibility of the task, tempers the industrial hubris.
When so much control fails and converts intended actions
into unintended consequences, there is a need to (re)consider
the place and role of humans in the cosmic scheme of things,
to take stock of the ways we approach finitude and the temporal limits to human being. Despite the very clear imperative, however, the reflective turn is *un*likely to come from
science or politics. The powerful agendas mentioned above
are potent disincentives to reflection. A more likely source is

the control/loss of control associated with the network society. Instantaneity and absolute connectivity expose the fault lines of the logic and confront users with entirely new temporal limits and possibilities that require the restructuring of socioeconomic relations. The social relations of time are central to this revision and renewal.

INTERLUDE

FUTURES

We tell futures
Druids & wizards
Oracles & prophets
Astrologers & palmists
Scientists and soothsayers
All but different means & modes

We know futures
From past experiences
Forecasts & forebodings
By prevision & premonitions
Through clairvoyance & intuition
To indeterminate degrees of certainty

We create futures
Through technology
Science & economics
For ourselves & others
Here & in distant locations
With no responsibility for effects

We colonize futures
With clock time values
And unintended outcomes
With econo-political impacts
And techno-scientific innovations
With impunity & freedom from redress

We eliminate futures
Our own & successors'
Through present-orientation
In politics, science and business
With the help of economic discounting
And no guardians to safeguard environments

We risk others' futures
Trading opportunity costs
For personal & political gain
Without being held to account
For potential harm to those affected
With no plans to protect new generations

Epilogue

At the end of this story we can see why the question 'What is time?' on its own is of little interest to social scientists. What time is, how it is conceptualized, what it means in practice, how the parameters set by nature are transcended across the ages, what changes are wrought by the quest for know-how and control, all these issues belong together. Collectively, they illuminate the wider picture and provide us with a basis from which to get a sense of the role of time in cultural existence in general and contemporary social life in particular. The conceptual re-presentation and construction of this temporal complexity, historically contextualized, is the task of social theory.

The conventional historical way to make sense of the changes is to tell sequential stories: first this, then that, followed by the next development, with each event-phenomenon located in an objective chronology. The traditional social science way, in contrast, is to impose dualistic categories on the complexity: traditional and modern, sacred and profane, natural and social, qualitative and quantitative time, to pick out just a few of the most prominent ones. Both traditions provide excellent means of illuminating difference and setting boundaries for the phenomena under investigation, but they leave unaddressed the relation of discontinuity to continuity, that is, continuity in the light of fundamental change, of change in relation to the past, and the influence of context on the merger of present and past. Imposition of chronology and categorization fragments the subject matter, abstracts it from both continuity and the larger picture and grounds the analysis in irreducible difference. Focus on difference, in turn, has the effect of losing sight of the power relations involved, both in the subject matter and in the creation of the subject matter: them and us, then and now, there and here. It fails to note that the 'us', the 'here' and the 'now' always take the unquestioned privileged position from which the subject is transformed into a distant object.

To categorize temporal relations and processes in dualistic terms engages theorists in boundary work, in establishing absolute distinctions, in active detemporalization of the subject matter. To categorize is to abstract from process, to fix and delimit, to construct otherness, to enforce either–or thinking. In the process of categorization theorists not only classify according to absolute criteria that eliminate what falls outside the definitional boundaries, they also render the thus excluded invisible. Lost are processes that bind levels of existence into a unified whole. Lost are practices as contextual process. Lost are difference and deviation from norms. Lost is any sense of negotiation and constructedness. Lost is the role of the theorist in the theory making. The anthropologist Johannes Fabian exposed the political nature of this tradition, showed the inherent distancing of subjects, their translation into objects and the denial of coevalness.[1]

The approach I have taken in this book (and in previous work) pursued a different agenda, took us into a number of alternative conceptual terrains. Focus on practices and temporal relations shifted the emphasis away from boundary work to engagement with processes and interdependencies. It opened the pores of encased subjects and softened the edges of bounded relations. It reanimated the ossified object, set it in motion. My intention throughout has been to minimize distance, to see together what conventional analysis had set apart. Through a variety of conceptual, literary and rhetorical devices I have sought to render the distant close and the strange familiar.

No matter where and how we were educated, so my reasoning goes, stories about creation and destiny, beginning and end, about a time before time and a time for redemption, about water, fire and the cycles of life and death, constitute the bedrock of how our elders have located us in the continuity of existence since time immemorial. Clearly the encounter with death has lost none of its pertinence and terror. The strategies to combat this most existential of concerns may differ between cultures and individuals but every one of us can recognize the fear of nothingness in the multitude of responses I have detailed in these pages. In our confrontation with temporality, so my argument goes, we find our common humanity.

With the spirit tempered by the encounter with death, we are open to the ancient stories and myths, to the projection of immortality on to gods and the comfort derived from rituals. Temporal distance across millennia evaporates as we recognize ourselves in the efforts to come to terms with the inescapability of the existential condition and to temper the effects of time, irrespective of when and where they occurred. Attempts to transcend finitude by cultural means permeate human existence. Differences in the modes of transcendence, as they were and are practised across time and space, can thus be located in the wider context of a common endeavour. Each move can be interpreted within this expanded frame of reference, each culturally based difference located in the pan-human quest, each distant past recognized for its place and relevance in the present.

To acknowledge the power of naming, accept the constructive nature of enquiry (scientific, historical, philosophical) and recognize the constitutive nature of knowledge is to understand social theory as a political endeavour: political in its processes of re-presentation and in its social consequences. From this perspective there is no innocent position from which to produce neutral knowledge, no objective realm from which to conduct acontextual investigations. Thus it deeply matters how we theorize the social relations of time past and present, their geneses and their projected futures. This is nowhere more pertinent than when we engage in analyses of the contemporary condition as theory intersects an open process and reflexively alters condition and outcome.

Notes

Part I   What is Time?

1   Time Stories

1   Re is also called Ra. As sun god Re is fused with Amun the hidden God and Atum the creator God, the perfect being, the complete one. Thus his name appears not just in the single form but also as Amun-Ra and Re-Atum. See Assmann, *The Search for God in Ancient Egypt*; Geddes & Grosset, *Ancient Egypt*; Hornung, *The Ancient Egyptian Books of the Afterlife*; and Littleton, *Mythology*, pp. 22–30.

2   Lippincott et al., *The Story of Time*, p. 3.

3   Ibid., pp. 32–3.

4   Ibid., p. 32.

5   Assmann, *The Search for God in Ancient Egypt*; Geddes & Grosset, *Ancient Egypt*; Hornung, *The Ancient Egyptian Books of the Afterlife*; Littleton, *Mythology*, pp. 26, 36.

6   Franz, *Time*, p. 6; Lippincott et al., *The Story of Time*, p. 38.

7   In Fagg, *The Becoming of Time*, the triple constellation is presented as Brahma the creator, Vishnu the preserver and Shiva the destroyer, driving the cosmic cycle as successive manifestations of the supreme Brahman (pp. 81, 221). Fagg suggests that the flexible Brahmanical tradition also allows for Vishnu to assume the three roles. See also Franz, *Time*, pp. 7 and 71, plates 31 and 27; Lippincott et al., *The Story of Time*, p. 25.

8   Franz, *Time*, pp. 8, 71.

9   See Wood, *The Celtic Book of Living and Dying*, p. 37.
10   In the cosmology of the Second Dynasty, Ptah was the first god and creator of Ra. He was coeval with the waters.
11   See Franz, *Time*, pp. 66–7; Littleton, *Mythology*, p. 139.
12   For the gods of chance and fortune, see Franz, *Time*, p. 25.
13   Quoted in Whitrow, *Time in History*, pp. 34–5.
14   See Dunne, *Time and Myth*, pp. 54–6; also Lippincott et al., *The Story of Time*, p. 22; Littleton, *Mythology*, pp. 84–6.
15   Quoted in Fagg, *The Becoming of Time*, p. 97, from Long, *Alpha*, p. 173, and Reanney, *The Death of Forever*, pp. 97, 99; also Littleton, *Mythology*, pp. 664–6.
16   Quoted in Reanney, *The Death of Forever*, pp. 98, 99.
17   The concept of 'dream time' was first used in the late nineteenth century by anthropologists who sought to make Aborigine culture comprehensible to Westerners. There is no one word for it but a set of concepts: the Yulngo 'wangarr', the Warlpiri 'tjukurrpa' and the Arrernte 'altyerrenge' are just three prominent examples of reference to an ancestral time-space that plays a central role in Aborigine present and future (Morphy, 'Australian Aboriginal Concepts of Time', p. 265).
18   Information drawn from Franz, *Time*, p. 94; Littleton, *Mythology*, pp. 646–9; Morphy, 'Australian Aboriginal Concepts of Time', pp. 264–7; Reanney, *The Death of Forever*, pp. 85–8.
19   Extracted from Dunne, *Time and Myth*, pp. 55–6.
20   This story is told in Ferguson, *The History of Myths Retold*, pp. 20–3; see also Littleton, *Mythology*, p. 279.
21   From the *Oxford Annotated Bible*, p. 1. The creation story of Islam does not differ significantly from the Judeo-Christian one.
22   From *New Jerusalem Bible*, p. 1744.
23   Rees, 'Understanding the Beginning and the End', p. 287.
24   The fine details may differ, but the story of a blissful beginning forms part of the mythology of cultures across the world – Aborigine and Maori, African, Amerindian, Aztec, Chinese, Egyptian, Greco-Latin, Indian, Iranian, Nordic, Tibetan – and of the major religions – Judaism, Christianity, Buddhism, Hinduism and Islam.
25   Mbiti, in *African Religions and Philosophy*, cites a great number of those conditions as told in the myths of African tribes: 'Bambuti were forbidden to look at God; the Banyarwanda were forbidden to hide death which God was hunting, the Bartose were forbidden to eat animals which

should have been their brothers; the Pare were forbidden to eat eggs and the Chagga forbidden to eat one type of yam (*ula*)' (p. 97).

26 The apple is a magical fruit in the myths of many cultures, among them Greek, Celtic, Gypsy. For the Myth of the Golden Apples of Idun, see Ferguson, *The History of Myths Retold*, pp. 72–5; Littleton, *Mythology*, p. 308.

27 This story which dates from *c*.2000 BC, is preserved on twelve clay tablets. Its title and first line, 'Sa nagba imuru', are variously translated as, for example, 'He Who Knew All Things' or 'He Who Saw Everything' (Dunne, *The City of the Gods*; Dunne, *Time and Myth*; Ferguson, *The History of Myths Retold*; Littleton, *Mythology*, pp. 116–33; Pritchard, *Ancient Near Eastern Texts*).

28 Quoted in Reanney, *The Death of Forever*, p. 93.

29 See Littleton, *Mythology*, pp. 42–3, 50–5; Reanney, *The Death of Forever*, pp. 104–5.

30 Homer's *Odyssey*, trans. Murray; Dunne, *The City of the Gods*; Dunne, *Time and Myth*; Littleton, *Mythology*, pp. 228–34.

31 Dunne, *Time and Myth*, p. 20.

32 The poet Dante Alighieri (1265–1321) lived and worked in Florence at a time of great social change and renewal.

33 Dante's *Inferno*, Canto XXIV lines 46–51, quoted in Macey, *Encyclopedia of Time*, p. 154.

34 Quoted in Dunne, *Time and Myth*, p. 29.

35 See Ferguson, *The History of Myths Retold*, pp. 52–3; Littleton, *Mythology*, p. 551.

36 This myth is recounted in Ferguson, *The History of Myths Retold*, pp. 112–15; see also Littleton, *Mythology*, pp. 96, 103.

37 For this Greek myth, see Ferguson, *The History of Myths Retold*, pp. 120–3; Graves, *The Greek Myths*, pp. 91–8; Littleton, *Mythology*, pp. 162–5.

38 See Ferguson, *The History of Myths Retold*, pp. 36–7; also Littleton, *Mythology*, p. 340.

39 Matthew 28, *Oxford Annotated Bible*, p. 1212.

40 Revelation 20–2, *New Jerusalem Bible*, pp. 2049–51.

41 I use the word spirit rather than mind to steer away from scientific mind-brain associations and to retain the mind-spirit connection that is expressed through the German concept of *Geist*.

42 For the most explicitly formulated exposition of this theory, see Dawkins, *The Blind Watchmaker*.

43 Reanney, *The Death of Forever*, p. 244.

2   Time Theories I

1   In addition to primary texts, my account of the classical philosophers' approaches to time draws on Jaspers, *The Great Philosophers*; Russell, *History of Western Philosophy*; A. Weber, *History of Philosophy*; Whitrow, *Time in History*.

2   Aristotle, *Physics*, Book IV, extracted in Gale, *The Philosophy of Time*, p. 15; also quoted in Whitrow, *Time in History*, p. 43.

3   Aristotle, *Physics*, Book IV, extracted in Gale, *The Philosophy of Time*, p. 17.

4   Ibid., p. 18.

5   Ibid., p. 21.

6   Thompson, 'Time, Work-Discipline and Industrial Capitalism', p. 57.

7   Adam, *Time and Social Theory*.

8   Quoted in Shallis, *On Time*, p. 17, and Zohar, *Through the Time Barrier*, p. 115.

9   Denbigh, *Three Concepts of Time*, p. 4.

10 Prigogine, *The End of Certainty*; Prigogine and Stengers, *Order out of Chaos*.

11 A. Weber, *History of Philosophy*, p. 357.

12 Jaspers, *The Great Philosophers*, p. 420.

13 Hegel, *Phaenomenologie des Geistes*, p. 558, my translation. *Geist* is variably translated as mind or spirit. I prefer to use spirit since, as far as I understand Hegel's theory, spirit is the next level, the dialectical synthesis of mind and body.

14 Hegel, *The Philosophy of Nature*, p. 230.

15 Ibid., p. 231.

16 Ibid.

17 As I discovered in secondary texts that focused explicitly on time in Hegel's work such as Gosden, *Social Being and Time*; Heidegger, *Being and Time*; Kirkland, 'Hegel, Georg Wilhelm Friedrich'; Mays, 'Temporality and Time in Hegel and Marx'.

18 Marx, *Grundrisse*, p. 140.

19 On the issue of commodified time, see also Giddens, *A Contemporary Critique of Historical Materialism*, pp. 118–20, 130–5; Harvey, *The Condition of Postmodernity*; Ingold, 'Work, Time and Industry'.

20 It was prefigured in Marx's 1844 *Economic and Philosophical Manuscripts*, as well as his 1857 *Grundrisse*.

21 Marx, *Capital, Volume I*, p. 534.

22 Ibid., p. 542.

23 Franklin, 'Necessary Hints to Those that would be Rich', p. 80, quoted in M. Weber, *The Protestant Ethic and the Spirit of Capitalism*, pp. 48–50.
24 M. Weber, *The Protestant Ethic and the Spirit of Capitalism*, pp. 118–19. Social scientists, such as Lewis Mumford (*The Human Prospect*) and Eviator Zerubavel (*Hidden Rhythms*), writing later on this theme, concentrated exclusively on the Benedictine monks for their elaborations on these connections.
25 M. Weber, *The Protestant Ethic and the Spirit of Capitalism*, pp. 118–19, 154.
26 Ibid., p. 124.
27 Albrow, *Max Weber's Construction of Social Theory*.
28 H. Hubert published his essay 'Étude sommaire de la représentation du temps dans la religion et la magie' (in English as *Essay on Time*) in 1905, M. Mauss wrote a critique and both essays were published in 1909 as *Mélanges d'histoire des religions*. Durkheim gave a first lecture course on religion in 1894–5 and he lectured on 'The Elementary Forms of Religious life' in 1900–1 and again on 'Religious Origins' in 1906–7 (Lukes, *Émile Durkheim*). He published *The Elementary Forms of Religious Life* in 1912; the first English translation was published in 1915.
29 Durkheim, *The Elementary Forms of Religious Life*, p. 9.
30 Ibid., pp. 18–19. I will come back to this statement in the next chapter when I discuss Mead's response to the same question.

3 Time Theories II

1 Plotinus, Third Ennead, Seventh Tractate, sections 7–13, extracted in Gale, *The Philosophy of Time*, pp. 30–7, here at p. 30.
2 Ibid., pp. 31, 33, 37.
3 St Augustine, *Confessions*, Book XI, extracted in Gale, *The Philosophy of Time*, p. 45. In the translation by Dodds, extracted in Bourke, *The Essential Augustine*, p. 234, this same passage is translated as: 'My mind burns with eagerness to gain knowledge of this complicated problem . . .'
4 St Augustine, *Confessions*, Book XI, extracted in Gale, *The Philosophy of Time*, p. 39.
5 St Augustine, *The City of God*, Book XI, 5–6, extracted in Bourke, *The Essential Augustine*, p. 109.

6   St Augustine, *Confessions*, Book XI, extracted in Bourke, *The Essential Augustine*, p. 242.

7   His most quoted passage on the matter is extracted in Bourke, *The Essential Augustine*, pp. 228–9, and in Gale, *The Philosophy of Time*, p. 40.

8   St Augustine, *Confessions*, Book XI, quoted in Jaques, *The Form of Time*, p. 5.

9   Kierkegaard, *The Concept of Dread*, quoted in Dreyfus, 'Human Temporality', p. 151, and Fagg, *The Becoming of Time*, p. 178.

10 Dreyfus, 'Human Temporality', p. 151.

11 Bergson's major theories of time are to be found in his *Time and Free Will* (1889), *Matter and Memory* (1896) and *Creative Evolution* (1907).

12 Game, *Undoing the Social*, p. 95.

13 Bergson, *Creative Evolution*, pp. 48–9.

14 Phenomenology was a much-used philosophical concept before Husserl developed it as a systematic method of scientific inquiry.

15 Perry, *Philosophy since 1860*, p. 586.

16 Husserl, *The Phenomenology of Internal Time Consciousness*, p. 110

17 Gosden, *Social Being and Time*, p. 108.

18 Heidegger, *Being and Time*, pp. 426–7.

19 Whitehead, *An Enquiry Concerning Principles of Natural Knowledge*, p. 17.

20 Whitehead, *Process and Reality*, p. 32.

21 Adam, *Time and Social Theory*.

22 Barnett, *The Universe and Dr Einstein*, p. 41.

23 Adam, *Time and Social Theory*.

24 Capra, *The Turning Point*, p. 75.

25 Ibid., p. 83.

26 On the importance of Mead's time theory see also Adam, *Time and Social Theory* and *Timewatch*; Bergmann, 'The Problem of Time in Sociology'; Eames, 'Mead's Concept of Time'; Flaherty and Fine, 'Present, Past and Future'; Giddens, *Central Problems in Social Theory*; Luhmann, 'World-Time and System History'; Joas, *G. H. Mead*.

27 Mead, *The Philosophy of the Present*, pp. 19–20.

28 Ibid., p. 1.

29 Ibid., p. 22.

30 In his later work Bergson too moved towards this conceptualization, see Capek, *Bergson and Modern Physics*, pp. 190–4.

31 Schutz, *The Problem of Social Reality*, pp. 172–3.

Part II   What is the Role of Time in Social Life?

1   Gosden, *Social Being and Time*, pp. 34–5.
2   E. Becker, *The Denial of Death*, p. ix.
3   Heidegger, *Being and Time*, p. 427.

4   *Cultural Practices of Time Transcendence*

1   Gosden, *Social Being and Time*, p. 9.
2   The work of Evans-Pritchard (*The Nuer*), Lévi-Strauss (*Structural Anthropology*) and Whorf (*Language, Thought and Reality*) can serve as prime exemplars for this approach; see Adam, 'Perceptions of Time'.
3   I have written on this classical perspective and argued extensively against this position. For more detailed discussions see Adam, *Time and Social Theory*; 'Perceptions of Time'; *Timewatch*.
4   Reanney, *The Death of Forever*, p. xxi.
5   Eliade, *The Myth of Eternal Return*, p. xii. Eliade designates myths 'exemplary models', 'paradigms' and 'archetypes'. To avoid conceptual confusion with the very different meanings given to the concepts by Thomas Kuhn and C. G. Jung respectively I will avoid the terms paradigms and archetypes.
6   Ibid., pp. 6, 21.
7   Ibid., p. 34.
8   The emphasis is on origin rather than the beginning since only origin can be 'enpresenced'.
9   Eliade uses both 'abolished' and 'suspended' (*The Myth of Eternal Return*, p. 35) and I wonder whether we are encountering here a problem of translation since only suspension of profane time seems to me to be appropriate to the processes in question. He also uses the term 'annulment', which I find as problematic as abolishment. The German *Aufhebung* with its triple meaning would be a very helpful concept here: ceasing/stopping/getting rid of, safe-keeping out of sight, and lifting to a higher level (see chapter 2).
10   Dossey, *Space, Time and Medicine*, pp. 28–31.
11   For these thoughts on monumental architecture I draw primarily on the work of Critchlow, *Time Stands Still*, who has written most perceptively on the temporality of megaliths and Neolithic artefacts.
12   Critchlow, *Time Stands Still*, p. 151.
13   Cohen, *Behaviour in Uncertainty*.
14   Black, *Nostradamus*.

15 Assmann, *The Search for God in Ancient Egypt*, p. 35.
16 See ibid.; Geddes & Grosset, *Ancient Egypt*; Hornung, *The Ancient Egyptian Books of the Afterlife*; Littleton, *Mythology*.
17 Based on much earlier coffin texts from the Sixth Dynasty, about 2658–2185 BC.
18 While in the old kingdom the transfer to eternity was the preserve of pharaohs, in later times it was open to anyone who could afford the rituals necessary for safe passage.
19 Littleton, *Mythology*, p. 185.
20 In Nordic myths too there is a strong tendency for prophecies to come true no matter how hard gods and mortals try to avert the destiny thus prophesied. In the myth of 'The Death of Balder the Beautiful', even the all-powerful Odin, god of light, and his wife, Frigg, are unable to prevent the killing of their son, as foretold in the prophecy (Ferguson, *The History of Myths Retold*, pp. 38–43; also Littleton, *Mythology*, pp. 286–93).
21 Littleton, *Mythology*, p. 223.
22 Zohar, *Through the Time Barrier*, p. 16.
23 Quoted in ibid., p. 18.
24 It was C. G. Jung's interest in the *I China* that opened it up to the West, and his writings on Synchronicity that explained the difference between causal thought and the understanding of significant coincidences. See Jung, *Synchronicity*; Franz, *Number and Time*; Franz, *Time*; Franz, *On Divination and Synchronicity*.
25 Jung, *Collected Works*, vol. 1, pp. iii–iv, quoted in Franz, *Time*, pp. 26–7.
26 It is however in tune with some of the basic tenets of quantum physics, as outlined in chapter 3. On the similarities with and differences from quantum physics see, for example, Capra, *The Tao of Physics*, and Zohar, *Through the Time Barrier*.
27 We know about the earliest human cultures because they left records of their activities. Archaeological records suggest that they buried their dead, harnessed fire, used tools and created artefacts and architecture. Each of these marks of culture encompasses specific temporal relations and particular engagements with finitude and transience. For archaeological records of approaches to time see Gosden, *Social Being and Time*.
28 For an overview of time in the major religions, see Balslev and Mohanty, *Religion and Time*; Fagg, *The Becoming of Time*, chs 6 and 12; relevant chapters in Macey, *Encyclopedia of Time*; and for Christian thought see Russell, *History of Western Philosophy*.

29   See Balslev, *A Study of Time in Indian Philosophy*; Hopkins, *The Hindu Religious Tradition*; Fagg, *The Becoming of Time*, chs 6 and 12.

30   Note the parallels with quantum physics, outlined in chapter 3, and Capra's suggestion that 'There is motion but there are, ultimately, no moving objects; there is activity but there are no actors; there are no dancers, there is only the dance' (*The Turning Point*, p. 83). For Buddhist approaches to time see Balslev, *A Study of Time in Indian Philosophy*; also Macey, *Encyclopedia of Time*.

31   See also St Augustine (chapter 3) who is considered to be the principal theorist of Christian time.

32   Goodman, 'Time in Islam', p. 139, quoted in Fagg, *The Becoming of Time*, p. 89.

33   There is evidence of burial, for example, from the megalithic period on the Scottish islands of Orkney and Arran, in Wales and Brittany, from the early Bronze Age in Denmark and Turkey, from the Neolithic period in the Outer Hebrides of Scotland and the South of England.

34   Barrett, Bradley and Green, *Landscape, Monuments and Society*.

35   Gosden, *Social Being and Time*, p. 88.

36   Mbiti, *African Religions and Philosophy*, pp. 149–66.

37   Plato, *Epinomis*, 991E1-4, quoted in Critchlow, *Time Stands Still*, p. 51.

38   For the background information to my argument I draw exclusively on Keith Critchlow's chapter 'Platonic Spheres – a Millennium before Plato', in *Time Stands Still*, pp. 131–49.

39   Ibid., p. 132.

40   Ibid., p. 145.

41   Plato, *The Timaeus, and the Critias*, pp. 173–5, cited in Critchlow, *Time Stands Still*, ch. 7.

42   For those two myths in particular, see Ferguson, *The History of Myths Retold*, pp. 66–9.

43   Eliade, *The Myth of Eternal Return*, pp. 28–9.

44   For the temporalities of text, image and film see Gross, 'Reading Time'.

45   Van Gennep, *The Rites of Passage*.

5   In Pursuit of Time Know-how

1   For a detailed analysis of the history of culture from archaic via magical and mythological to mental and integrated systems of existence, see the two-volume work of Jean Gebser, *The Ever-Present Origin*.

2   Coser and Coser, 'Time Perspective in Social Structure'; Elias, *Time*; Jaques, *The Form of Time*; Lauer, *Temporal Man*; Lewis and Weigert, 'Structures and Meanings of Social Time'; Nowotny, 'Time Structuring and Time Measurement'; Sorokin, *Sociocultural Causality, Space and Time*; Sorokin and Merton, 'Social Time'; Zerubavel, *Hidden Rhythms*; Zerubavel, *The Seven Day Circle*.

3   Elias, *Time*, pp. 6, 8.

4   For detailed analyses and histories of calendar systems from across the world, see Landes, *Revolution in Time*; Richards, *Mapping Time*; Borst, *The Ordering of Time*. For general introductions, see Macey, *Encyclopedia of Time*, entries under Archaeoastronomy, Archaeology and Time's Measurements and Divisions, as well as Lippincott et al., *The Story of Time*, pp. 30–169.

5   Aveni, *Archaeoastronomy in Pre-Columbian America*; Aveni, *Skywatchers of Ancient Mexico*; Aveni, 'Archaeoastronomy'; Heggie, *Archaeoastronomy in the Old World*; Ruggles, *Megalithic Astronomy*; Ruggles, *Records in Stone*; Ruggles, 'British Archaeoastronomy'.

6   See also chapter 4 on the cultural time practices of transcendence, especially the sections on monumental architecture and the carved stone spheres of Neolithic Britain.

7   See Ruggles, 'British Archaeoastronomy', pp. 68–9, and on the changing relation to death see also Gosden, *Social Being and Time*, esp. ch. 5.

8   Zerubavel, *The Seven Day Circle*, p. 31.

9   Durkheim, *The Elementary Forms of Religious Life*, p. 23.

10   See Eliade, *The Sacred and the Profane*; Leach, *Rethinking Anthropology*; Lévi-Strauss, *The Savage Mind*.

11   Durkheim, *The Elementary Forms of Religious Life*.

12   For information on Maya and Mesoamerican calendars and chronology see, for example, Aveni, *Skywatchers of Ancient Mexico*; Closs, 'Maya Calendars and Chronology', pp. 364–9; Thompson, 'Maya Astronomy', pp. 83–98.

13   For cultural variations on the week, see Zerubavel, *The Seven Day Circle*, esp. ch. 3.

14   On time in India, see Lippincott et al., *The Story of Time*, pp. 42–8.

15   For transcendence of seasonal cycles, see also chapter 4.

16   Landes, *Revolution in Time*, p. 33.

17   For details of these two fascinating attempts to change the calendar, see Zerubavel, *The Seven Day Circle*, ch. 2.

18   For information on Japan's Westernization of time, see Nishimoto, 'The "Civilization" of Time', pp. 237–60.

19 Mumford, *The Human Prospect*, p. 3.
20 Landes, *Revolution in Time*, p. 17.
21 Mumford, *The Human Prospect*, p. 9.
22 For work detailing that slow development see Thrift, 'Owners' Time and Own Time' and 'Vicos Voco'.
23 Landes, *Revolution in Time*, pp. 59–64.
24 M. Weber, *The Protestant Ethic and the Spirit of Capitalism*.
25 For example by the historians Landes, *Revolution in Time*, and Le Goff, *Time, Work and Culture in the Middle Ages*, as well as the social scientists Mumford, *The Human Prospect*, and Zerubavel, *Hidden Rhythms*, ch. 2.
26 Landes, *Revolution in Time*, p. 60.
27 Ibid., p. 93.
28 Mumford, *The Human Prospect*, p. 5.
29 See Bartky, *Selling the True Time*, for a detailed historical account of the establishment of standard railway time in North America.
30 For a documentary novel on the subject see Sobel, *Longitude*, and for a brief account of the entire history see Andrewes, 'Longitude', pp. 346–50; also Landes, *Revolution in Time*.
31 Andrewes, 'Longitude', p. 346.
32 Kern, *The Culture of Time and Space 1880–1919*.
33 Ibid., pp. 66–8.

6 The Quest for Time Control

1 Some of this chapter's material has been researched for two recently completed journal articles: Adam, 'The Gendered Time Politics of Globalisation' and 'Reflexive Modernisation Temporalised'. A certain amount of overlap with that work is therefore unavoidable.
2 M. Weber, *The Protestant Ethic and the Spirit of Capitalism*.
3 This perspective also applies to Islam but not to Judaism. The difference was one important reason why the time merchants of the Middle Ages were predominantly Jewish traders.
4 See Le Goff, *Time, Work and Culture in the Middle Ages*, especially his illuminating part 1 on 'Time and Labour'.
5 Ibid., p. 30.
6 For further detail see ibid., pp. 29–100.
7 Franklin, 'Necessary Hints to Those that would be Rich', quoted in M. Weber, *The Protestant Ethic and the Spirit of Capitalism*, pp. 48–50.
8 Schultz, *Der erregende Mythos vom Geld*, p. 193.
9 For examples of such an approach, see Adam, *Timescapes of Modernity* and 'The Gendered Time Politics of Globalisation'.

10　Rifkin, *Time Wars*, pp. 3–4.
11　Harvey, *The Condition of Postmodernity*.
12　Kern, *The Culture of Time and Space 1880–1919*.
13　Marinetti (1909) in Apollonio, *Futurist Manifestos*, pp. 1–24.
14　Marinetti (1909) in Flint, *Marinetti*, p. 41.
15　For my outline of Virilio's work on speed I draw on a number of publications: Virilio's exhibition catalogue *La Vitesse*, and two of his translated books, *The Art of the Motor* and *Open Sky*.
16　For a detailed cultural analysis of these changes, see Kern, *The Culture of Time and Space 1880–1919*.
17　See, for example, Whitelegg, *Transport for a Sustainable Future*; Whitelegg, *Critical Mass*.
18　Virilio, *La Vitesse*; *Open Sky*.
19　Rifkin and Howard, *Entropy*, p. 264.
20　Virilio, *La Vitesse*, p. 65.
21　Virilio, *Open Sky*. In contrast to Virilio, Zygmunt Bauman writes about 'dephysicalization' where the power holders of global finance and cyberspace, for example, become truly exterritorial, even extraterrestrial (*Globalization*, p. 19).
22　Virilio, *Open Sky*, pp. 10–11.
23　Virilio, *The Art of the Motor*, p. 85.
24　Virilio, *Open Sky*, p. 20.
25　Bauman, *Globalization*, pp. 8–9.
26　Virilio, *The Art of the Motor*, p. 99.
27　Ibid., p. 100.
28　Ibid., p. 123.
29　Castells, *The Rise of the Network Society*, p. 461.
30　Ibid., p. 464.
31　Ibid., p. 463.
32　Hassan, 'Network Time and the New Knowledge Epoch', p. 234.
33　Ibid., p. 235.
34　Beck, 'The Politics of Risk Society', p. 15.
35　Adam, 'The Gendered Time Politics of Globalisation'.
36　Melbin, *Night as Frontier*; Kern, *The Culture of Time and Space 1880–1919*.
37　A particularly powerful account of such an occasion is given in Raymond Murphy's 'Nature's Temporalities and the Manufacture of Vulnerability', an essay on the temporality of an unusually fierce winter ice storm in Canada which, in some cases, left people without electricity and heating for over one week.
38　For the creation of clock time see chapter 5, for commodification and compression see the earlier sections in this chapter, for the (re)formulation in Newtonian science see chapters 2 and 3.

39 The material in this box is replicated from Adam, 'Reflexive Modernisation Temporalised'.
40 On the subject of disembedded time see also Giddens, especially *The Consequences of Modernity*.
41 For an expanded argument, see Adam, *Time and Social Theory*, pp. 138–48, and *Timescapes of Modernity*.
42 G. S. Becker, 'A Theory of the Allocation of Time'; Sharp, *The Economics of Time*.
43 I have already alluded to a similar distinction in chapter 4 where I was explaining the difference in time arresting and eliminating practices by contrasting the performance of a ritual with listening to a Beethoven piano concerto on a compact disc.
44 See for example the classic work of Shackle, *Time in Economics*.
45 Giddens, *Reith Lecture 2: Risk*, p. 2.
46 For an economic treatise on discounting, see Price, *Time, Discounting and Value*. For a brief socio-environmental comment on the practice, see Adam, *Timescapes of Modernity*.
47 Nowotny, *Time*.
48 Serres, *Genesis*, p. 93.
49 Castells, *The Rise of the Network Society*.
50 Poster, *The Mode of Information*, p. 3.
51 For a more detailed argument on this subject, see Adam, *Timescapes of Modernity* and 'The Temporal Gaze'; Kollek, 'The Limits of Experimental Knowledge'.
52 Beck, 'The Reinvention of Politics'.

Epilogue

1 Fabian, *Time and the Other*; Fabian, *Time and the Work of Anthropology*.

Further Reading

B. Adam, *Time and Social Theory*. Cambridge: Polity, 1990.

B. Adam, *Timewatch: The Social Analysis of Time*. Cambridge: Polity, 1995.

B. Adam, *Timescapes of Modernity: The Environment and Invisible Hazards*. London: Routledge, 1998.

A. C. Bluedorn, *The Human Organization of Time: Temporal Realities and Experience*. Stanford: Stanford University Press, 2002.

K. Critchlow, *Time Stands Still: A New Light on Megalithic Science*. London: Gordon Fraser, 1979.

K. Daly, *Families and Time: Keeping Pace in a Hurried Culture*. London: Sage, 1996.

K. Davies, *Women and Time: Weaving the Strands of Everyday Life*. Aldershot: Avebury, 1990.

J. S. Dunne, *Time and Myth: A Meditation on Storytelling as an Exploration of Life and Death* (1973). London: SCM Press, 1979.

M. Eliade, *The Myth of Eternal Return: Cosmos and History* (1949). London: Arkana, 1989.

N. Elias, *Time: An Essay*. Oxford: Blackwell, 1992.

J. Fabian, *Time and the Other: How Anthropology Makes its Object*. New York: Columbia University Press, 1983.

L. Fagg, *The Becoming of Time*. Atlanta: Scholars Press, 1995.

J. T. Fraser, *Time the Familiar Stranger*. Amherst: University of Massachusetts Press, 1987.

R. M. Gale (ed.), *The Philosophy of Time* (1968). Brighton: Harvester Press, 1978.

A. Gell, *The Anthropology of Time: Cultural Constructions of Temporal Maps and Images*. Oxford: Berg, 1992.

C. Gosden, *Social Being and Time*. Oxford: Blackwell, 1994.

J. Griffiths, *Pip Pip: A Sideways Look at Time*. London: Flamingo, 2000.

J. Hassard (ed.), *The Sociology of Time*. Basingstoke: Macmillan, 1990.

S. Kern, *The Culture of Time and Space 1880–1919*. London: Weidenfeld & Nicolson, 1983.

D. S. Landes, *Revolution in Time*. Cambridge: Harvard University Press, 1983.

J. Le Goff, *Time, Work and Culture in the Middle Ages*. Chicago: University of Chicago Press, 1980.

K. Lippincott, U. Eco, E. H. Gombrich et al., *The Story of Time*. London: Merrell Holberton, 1999.

S. L. Macey (ed.), *Encyclopedia of Time*. New York: Garland, 1994.

G. H. Mead, *The Philosophy of the Present* (1932), ed. A. E. Murphy, preface by John Dewey. Chicago: University of Chicago Press, 1980.

M. Melbin, *Night as Frontier: Colonizing the World after Dark*. New York: Free Press, 1987.

W. E. Moore, *Man, Time and Society*. New York: John Wiley & Son, 1963.

H. Nowotny, *Time: The Modern and Postmodern Experience* (1989), trans. N. Plaice. Cambridge: Polity, 1994.

M. O'Malley, *Keeping Watch: A History of American Time*. New York: Viking/Penguin, 1990.

J. Rifkin, *Time Wars*. New York: Henry Holt, 1987.

M. Shallis, *On Time: An Investigation into Scientific Knowledge and Human Experience*. Harmondsworth: Penguin, 1983.

C. Sharp, *The Economics of Time*. Oxford: Martin Robertson, 1981.

D. Sobel, *Longitude*. London: Fourth Estate, 1995.

P. A. Sorokin, *Sociocultural Causality, Space and Time: A Study of Referential Principles of Sociology and Social Science*. New York: Russell & Russell, 1964.

H. G. Wells, *The Time Machine* (1895). London: Pan Books, 1980.

M. Young, *The Metronomic Society: Natural Rhythms and Human Timetables*. Cambridge: Harvard University Press, 1988.

M. Young and T. Schuller (eds), *The Rhythms of Society*, London: Routledge & Kegan Paul, 1988.

E. Zerubavel, *Hidden Rhythms: Schedules and Calendars in Social Life*. Chicago: University of Chicago Press, 1981.

Bibliography

Adam, B., *Time and Social Theory*. Cambridge: Polity, 1990.

Adam, B., 'Perceptions of Time'. In T. Ingold (ed.), *Companion Encyclopedia of Anthropology: Humanity, Culture and Social Life*, London: Routledge, 1994, pp. 503–27.

Adam, B., *Timewatch: The Social Analysis of Time*. Cambridge: Polity, 1995.

Adam, B., *Timescapes of Modernity: The Environment and Invisible Hazards*. London: Routledge, 1998.

Adam, B., 'The Temporal Gaze: The Challenge for Social Theory in the Context of GM Food'. *British Journal of Sociology*, 51 (2000), pp. 125–42.

Adam, B., 'The Gendered Time Politics of Globalisation: Of Shadowlands and Elusive Justice'. *Feminist Review*, 70 (2002), pp. 3–29.

Adam, B., 'Reflexive Modernisation Temporalised'. *Theory, Culture & Society*, 20, no. 2 (2003), pp. 59–78.

Albrow, M., *Max Weber's Construction of Social Theory*. London: Macmillan, 1990.

Andrewes, W. J. H., 'Longitude'. In S. L. Macey (ed.), *Encyclopedia of Time*, New York: Garland Publishing, 1994, pp. 346–50.

Apollonio, U. (ed.), *Futurist Manifestos*. London and New York: Thames & Hudson, 1973.

Assmann, J., *The Search for God in Ancient Egypt* (1984), trans. David Lorton. Ithaca and London: Cornell University Press, 2001.

Aveni, A. F., *Skywatchers of Ancient Mexico*. Austin: University of Texas Press, 1980.

Aveni, A. F., 'Archaeoastronomy'. In S. L. Macey (ed.), *Encyclopedia of Time*. New York: Garland Publishing, 1994, pp. 26–35.

Aveni, A. F. (ed.), *Archaeoastronomy in Pre-Columbian America*. Austin: University of Texas Press, 1975.

Balslev, A. N., *A Study of Time in Indian Philosophy*. Wiesbaden: Otto Harrassowitz, 1983.

Balslev, A. N. and Mohanty, J. N. (eds), *Religion and Time*. New York: E. J. Brill, 1993.

Barnett, L., *The Universe and Dr Einstein*. New York: William Sloane, 1957.

Barrett, J., Bradley, R. and Green, M., *Landscape, Monuments and Society*. Cambridge: Cambridge University Press, 1991.

Bartky, I. R., *Selling the True Time: Nineteenth-Century Timekeeping in America*. Stanford: Stanford University Press, 2000.

Bauman, Z., *Globalization: The Human Consequences*. Cambridge: Polity, 1998.

Beck, U., 'The Reinvention of Politics: Towards a Theory of Reflexive Modernization'. In U. Beck, A. Giddens and S. Lash, *Reflexive Modernization*, Cambridge: Polity, 1994, pp. 1–55.

Beck, U., 'The Politics of Risk Society'. In J. Franklin (ed.), *The Politics of Risk Society*, Cambridge: Polity, 1998, pp. 9–22.

Beck, U., 'Risk Society Revisited: Theory, Politics and Research Programmes'. In B. Adam, U. Beck and J. van Loon (eds), *The Risk Society and Beyond: Critical Issues for Social Theory*, London: Sage, 2000, pp. 211–29.

Becker, E., *The Denial of Death*. New York: Macmillan, 1973.

Becker, G. S., 'A Theory of the Allocation of Time'. *Economic Journal*, 299 (1965), pp. 495–517.

Bergmann, W., 'The Problem of Time in Sociology: An Overview of the Literature on the State of Theory and Research on the "Sociology of Time", 1900–82'. *Time and Society*, 1, no. 1 (1992), pp. 81–134.

Bergson, H., *Time and Free Will* (1889), trans. F. L. Pogson. New York: Harper & Row, 1960.

Bergson, H., *Matter and Memory* (1896), trans. N. M. Paul and W. S. Palmer. New York: Zone Books, 1991.

Bergson, H., *Creative Evolution* (1907), trans. A. Mitchell. Lanham: University Press of America, 1983.

Borst, A., *The Ordering of Time: From the Ancient Computus to the Modern Computer*, trans. A. Winnard. Cambridge: Polity, 1993.

Bourke, V. J. (ed.), *The Essential Augustine*. Indianapolis: Hackett, 1983.

Black, A. J., *Nostradamus: The Prophesies*. Leicester: Abbeydale Press, 2002.

Capek, M., *The Philosophical Impact of Contemporary Physics.* Princeton: D. van Nostrand, 1961.

Capek, M., *Bergson and Modern Physics.* Dordrecht: Reidel, 1971.

Capra, F., *The Tao of Physics.* London: Fontana, 1976.

Capra, F., *The Turning Point.* London: Wildwood House, 1982.

Castells, M., *The Rise of the Network Society.* Oxford: Blackwell, 1996.

Closs, M. P., 'Maya Calendars and Chronology'. In S. L. Macey (ed.), *Encyclopedia of Time*, New York: Garland, 1994, pp. 366–9.

Cohen, J., *Behaviour in Uncertainty.* London: Allen & Unwin, 1964.

Collins, G. W., II, 'Standard Time: Time Zones and Daylight Saving Time'. In S. L. Macey (ed.), *Encyclopedia of Time*, New York: Garland, 1994, pp. 575–7.

Coser, L. A. and Coser, R. L., 'Time Perspective in Social Structure'. In A. W. Gouldner and H. P. Gouldner (eds), *Modern Sociology: An Introduction to the Study of Human Interaction*, London: Rupert Hart Davis, 1963, pp. 638–51.

Critchlow, K., *Time Stands Still: A New Light on Megalithic Science.* London: Gordon Fraser, 1979.

Dawkins, R., *The Blind Watchmaker.* London: Penguin, 1988.

Denbigh, K. G., *Three Concepts of Time.* New York: Springer Verlag, 1981.

Dossey, L., *Space, Time and Medicine.* London: Shambala, 1982.

Dreyfus, H. L., 'Human Temporality'. In J. T. Fraser and N. Lawrence (eds), *The Study of Time II*, New York: Springer Verlag, 1975, pp. 150–62.

Dunne, J. S., *The City of the Gods.* New York: Macmillan, 1965.

Dunne, J. S., *Time and Myth: A Meditation on Storytelling as an Exploration of Life and Death* (1973). London: SCM Press, 1979.

Durkheim, É., *The Elementary Forms of Religious Life: A Study in Religious Sociology* (1912), trans. J. W. Swain. London: George Allen & Unwin, 1971.

Eames, E. R., 'Mead's Concept of Time'. In W. R. Corti (ed.), *The Philosophy of George Herbert Mead*, Winterthur: Amriswiler Bücherei, 1973, pp. 59–82.

Eliade, M., *The Myth of Eternal Return: Cosmos and History* (1949). London: Arkana, 1989.

Eliade, M., *The Sacred and the Profane.* New York: Harcourt, Brace & World, 1959.

Elias, N., *Time: An Essay.* Oxford: Blackwell, 1992.

Evans-Pritchard, E. E., *The Nuer.* Oxford: Oxford University Press, 1940.

Fabian, J., *Time and the Other: How Anthropology Makes its Object*. New York: Columbia University Press, 1983.

Fabian, J., *Time and the Work of Anthropology: Critical Essays 1971–1991*. Philadelphia: Harwood Academic, 1991.

Fagg, L., *The Becoming of Time*. Atlanta: Scholars Press, 1995.

Ferguson, D., *The History of Myths Retold*. London: Chancellor Press, 2000.

Flaherty, M. G. and Fine, G. A., 'Present, Past and Future: Conjugating George Herbert Mead's Perspective on Time'. *Time and Society*, 10, nos 2–3 (2001), pp. 147–62.

Flint, R. W. (ed.), *Marinetti: Selected Writings*. New York: Farrar, Straus & Giroux, 1971.

Franklin, B., 'Necessary Hints to Those that would be Rich'. In *Works*, Sparks Edition II, 1736.

Franz, M. L. von, *Number and Time*. London: Northwestern University Press, 1974.

Franz, M. L. von, *Time: Rhythm and Repose*. London: Thames & Hudson, 1978.

Franz, M. L. von, *On Divination and Synchronicity: The Psychology of Meaningful Chance*. Toronto: Inner City Books, 1980.

Gale, R. M. (ed.), *The Philosophy of Time* (1968). Brighton: Harvester Press, 1978.

Game, A., *Undoing the Social: Towards a Deconstructive Sociology*. Milton Keynes: Open University Press, 1991.

Gardner, M., *The Ambidextrous Universe* (1964). Harmondsworth: Penguin, 1982.

Gebser, J., *The Ever-Present Origin*, (2 vols, 1949 and 1953), trans. N. Barstad and A. Mickunas. Athens: Ohio University Press, 1985.

Geddes & Grosset, *Ancient Egypt: Myth and History*. New Lanark: Geddes & Grosset, 1997.

Giddens, A., *Central Problems in Social Theory: Action, Structure and Contradiction in Social Analysis*. London: Macmillan, 1979.

Giddens, A., *A Contemporary Critique of Historical Materialism: Power, Property and the State*. London: Macmillan, 1981.

Giddens, A., *The Consequences of Modernity*. Cambridge: Polity, 1990.

Giddens, A., *Reith Lecture 2: Risk*. London: BBC, 1999.

Goodman, L. E., 'Time in Islam'. In A. N. Balslev and J. N. Mohanty (eds), *Religion and Time*, New York: E. J. Brill, 1993, pp. 138–62.

Gosden, C., *Social Being and Time*. Oxford: Blackwell, 1994.

Graves, R., *The Greek Myths* (1955), vols 1 and 2. London: Folio Society, 1998.

Gross, S., 'Reading Time: Text, Image, Film'. *Time and Society*, 1, no. 2, (1992), pp. 207–22.

Harvey, D., *The Condition of Postmodernity*. Oxford: Blackwell, 1989.

Hassan, R., 'Network Time and the New Knowledge Epoch'. *Time and Society*, 12 (2003), pp. 225–41.

Hegel, G. W. F., *Phaenomenologie des Geistes* (1807). Hamburg: Felix Meiner Verlag, 1952.

Hegel, G. W. F., *The Philosophy of Nature* (1840), trans. M. J. Petry. London: George Allen & Unwin, 1970.

Heggie, D. (ed.), *Archaeoastronomy in the Old World*. Cambridge: Cambridge University Press, 1982.

Heidegger, M., *Being and Time* (1927), trans. J. Macquarrie and E. Robinson. Oxford: Blackwell, 1980.

Homer, *Odyssey*, trans. A. T. Murray. London: Heinemann, 1931.

Hopkins, T. J., *The Hindu Religious Tradition*. Belmont: Dickenson, 1971.

Hornung, E., *The Ancient Egyptian Books of the Afterlife* (1997), trans. David Lorton. Ithaca and London: Cornell University Press, 1999.

Hubert, H., 'Étude sommaire de la représentation du temps dans la religion et la magie'. *Annuaire de l'École Pratique des Hautes Études* (1905), pp. 1–39.

Hubert, H. and Mauss, M., *Mélanges d'histoire des religions*. Paris: Alcan, 1909.

Husserl, E., *The Phenomenology of Internal Time Consciousness* (1905–10), trans. S. Churchill. The Hague: Martinus Nijhoff, 1964.

Ingold, T., 'Work, Time and Industry'. *Time and Society*, 4, no. 1 (1995), pp. 5–28.

Jaques, E., *The Form of Time*. London: Heinemann, 1982.

Jaspers, K., *The Great Philosophers* (1957), ed. H. Arendt, trans. R. Manheim. London: Rupert Hart-Davis, 1962.

Joas, H., *G. H. Mead: A Contemporary Re-examination of his Thought*, trans. R. Meyer. Cambridge: Polity, 1985.

Jung, C. G., *Collected Works*, vol. 1, ed. H. Read. London: Routledge & Kegan Paul, 1961.

Jung, C. G., *Synchronicity*. London: Routledge, 1972.

Kant, I., *Critique of Pure Reason* (1848), trans. P. Guyer and A. W. Wood. Cambridge: Cambridge University Press, 1998.

Kern, S., *The Culture of Time and Space 1880–1919*. London: Weidenfeld & Nicolson, 1983.

Kirkland, F. M., 'Hegel, Georg Wilhelm Friedrich (1770–1831)'. In S. L. Macey (ed.), *Encyclopedia of Time*, New York: Garland, 1994, pp. 259–60.

Kollek, R., 'The Limits of Experimental Knowledge: A Feminist Perspective on the Ecological Risks of Genetic Engineering'. In V. Shiva and I. Moser (eds), *Biopolitics: A Feminist and Ecological Reader on Biotechnology*, London: Zed Books, 1995, pp. 95–111.

Landes, D. S., *Revolution in Time*. Cambridge: Harvard University Press, 1983.

Lauer, R. H., *Temporal Man: The Meaning and Uses of Social Time*. New York: Praeger, 1981.

Leach, E. R., *Rethinking Anthropology*. London: Athlone, 1961.

Le Goff, J., *Time, Work and Culture in the Middle Ages*. Chicago: University of Chicago Press, 1980.

Lévi-Strauss, C., *Structural Anthropology* (1963). Harmondsworth: Penguin, 1972.

Lévi-Strauss, C., *The Savage Mind*. Chicago: University of Chicago Press, 1966.

Lewis, J. D. and Weigert, A. J., 'Structures and Meanings of Social Time'. *Social Forces*, 60 (1981), pp. 433–62.

Lippincott, K., Eco, U., Gombrich, E. H. et al., *The Story of Time*. London: Merrell Holberton, 1999.

Littleton, S. C. (ed.), *Mythology*. London: Duncan Baird, 2002.

Lockyer, J. N., *The Dawn of Astronomy* (1894). Cambridge: MIT Press, 1964.

Long, C. H., *Alpha: The Myth of Creation*. New York: George Braziller, 1963.

Luhmann, N., 'World-Time and System History'. In N. Luhmann, *The Differentiation of Society*, New York: Columbia University Press, 1982, pp. 289–324.

Lukes, S., *Émile Durkheim: His Life and Work: A Historical and Critical Study*. Harmondsworth: Penguin, 1973.

Macey, S. L. (ed.), *Encyclopedia of Time*. New York: Garland, 1994.

Marx, K., *Economic and Philosophical Manuscripts* (1844). Moscow: Progress, 1977.

Marx, K., *Grundrisse* (1857). Harmondsworth: Penguin, 1973.

Marx, K., *Capital, Volume I* (1867). Harmondsworth: Penguin, 1976.

Mays, W., 'Temporality and Time in Hegel and Marx'. In J. T. Fraser and N. Lawrence (eds), *The Study of Time, Volume II*, New York: Springer Verlag, 1975, pp. 98–113.

Mbiti, J. S., *African Religions and Philosophy* (1969). London: Heinemann, 1985.

Mead, G. H., *The Philosophy of the Present* (1932), ed. A. E. Murphy, preface by John Dewey. Chicago: University of Chicago Press, 1980.

Melbin, M., *Night as Frontier: Colonizing the World after Dark*. New York: Free Press, 1987.

Morphy, H., 'Australian Aboriginal Concepts of Time'. In K. Lippincott et al., *The Story of Time*. London: Merrell Holberton, 1999, pp. 264–7.

Mumford, L., *The Human Prospect* (1934). Boston: Beacon Press, 1955.

Murphy, R., 'Nature's Temporalities and the Manufacture of Vulnerability: A Study of a Sudden Disaster with Implications for Creeping Ones'. *Time and Society*, 10, nos 2–3 (2001), pp. 329–48.

New Jerusalem Bible, revised edn (1973). London: Darton, Longman & Todd, 1985.

Newton, I., *The Principia* (1686–7), trans. A. Motte. New York: Prometheus Books, 1995.

Nishimoto, I., 'The "Civilization" of Time: Japan and the Adoption of the Western Time System'. *Time and Society*, 6, nos 2–3 (1997), pp. 237–60.

Nowotny, H., 'Time Structuring and Time Measurement: On the Interrelation between Time Keepers and Social Time'. In J. T. Fraser and N. Lawrence (eds), *The Study of Time II*, Berlin: Springer Verlag, 1975, pp. 325–42.

Nowotny, H., *Time: The Modern and Postmodern Experience* (1989), trans. N. Plaice. Cambridge: Polity, 1994.

Oxford Annotated Bible, revised standard edn (1946). Oxford: Oxford University Press, 1965.

Perry, R. B., *Philosophy since 1860* (1896). In A. Weber and R. B. Perry, *History of Philosophy, with Philosophy since 1860*, New York: Charles Scribner's Sons, 1925, pp. 458–594.

Plato, *The Timaeus, and the Critias, or Atlanticus*, trans. T. Taylor. New York: Pantheon, 1952.

Poster, M., *The Mode of Information: Poststructuralism and Social Context*. Cambridge: Polity, 1990.

Price, C., *Time, Discounting and Value*. Oxford: Blackwell, 1993.

Prigogine, I., *The End of Certainty: Time, Chaos and the New Laws of Nature*. New York: Free Press, 1997.

Prigogine, I. and Stengers, I., *Order out of Chaos*. London: Heinemann, 1984.

Pritchard, J. B., *Ancient Near Eastern Texts*. Princeton: Princeton University Press, 1955.

Reanney, D., *The Death of Forever: A New Future for Human Consciousness* (1991). London: Souvenir Press, 1995.

Rees, M., 'Understanding the Beginning and the End'. In K. Lippincott et al., *The Story of Time*, London: Merrell Holberton, 1999, pp. 284–95.

Richards, E. G., *Mapping Time: The Calendar and its History*. Oxford: Oxford University Press, 1998.

Rifkin, J., *Time Wars*. New York: Henry Holt, 1987.

Rifkin, J. and Howard, T., *Entropy: A New World View* (1980). London: Paladin, 1985.

Ruggles, C. L. N., *Megalithic Astronomy: A New Archaeological and Statistical Study of 300 Western Scottish Sites*. Oxford: British Archaeological Reports (British Series 123), 1984.

Ruggles, C. L. N., 'British Archaeoastronomy'. In S. L. Macey (ed.), *Encyclopedia of Time*, New York: Garland Publishing, 1994, pp. 68–9.

Ruggles, C. L. N. (ed.), *Records in Stone*. Cambridge: Cambridge University Press, 1988.

Russell, B., *History of Western Philosophy* (1946). London: George Allen & Unwin, 1981.

Russell, J. L., 'Time in Christian Thought' (1966). In J. T. Fraser (ed.), *The Voices of Time*, Amherst: University of Massachusetts Press, 1981, pp. 59–76.

Schultz, I., *Der erregende Mythos vom Geld. Die neue Verbindung von Zeit, Geld und Geschlecht im Ökologiezeitalter*. Frankfurt am Main: Campus, 1994.

Schutz, A., *The Problem of Social Reality, vol. 1 of Collected Papers*, ed. M. Natanson. The Hague: Martinus Nijhoff, 1971.

Serres, M., *Genesis* (1982). Michigan: University of Michigan Press, 1999.

Shackle, G. L. S., *Time in Economics*. Amsterdam: North Holland, 1967.

Shallis, M., *On Time: An Investigation into Scientific Knowledge and Human Experience*. Harmondsworth: Penguin, 1983.

Sharp, C., *The Economics of Time*. Oxford: Martin Robertson, 1981.

Sobel, D., *Longitude*. London: Fourth Estate, 1995.

Sorokin, P. A., *Sociocultural Causality, Space and Time: A Study of Referential Principles of Sociology and Social Science*. New York: Russell & Russell, 1964.

Sorokin, P. A. and Merton, R. K., 'Social Time: A Methodological and Functional Analysis'. *American Journal of Sociology*, 42 (1937), pp. 615–29.

Thom, A., *Megalithic Sites in Britain*. Oxford: Oxford University Press, 1967.

Thompson, E. P., 'Time, Work-Discipline and Industrial Capitalism'. *Past and Present*, 36 (1967), pp. 57–97.

Thompson, J. E. S., 'Maya Astronomy'. *Philosophical Transactions of the Royal Society of London*, 276 (1974), pp. 83–98.

Thrift, N., 'Owners' Time and Own Time: The Making of a Capitalist Time Consciousness, 1300–1800'. In A. R. Pred (ed.), *Space and Time in Geography*, Lund: Gleerup, 1981, pp. 56–84.

Thrift, N., 'Vicos Voco: Ringing the Changes in Historical Geography of Time Consciousness'. In M. Young and T. Schuller (eds), *The Rhythms of Society*, London: Routledge & Kegan Paul, 1988, pp. 53–94.

van Gennep, A., *The Rites of Passage*, trans. M. B. Vicedom and G. L. Caffee. Chicago: University of Chicago Press, 1960.

Virilio, P., *La Vitesse*, Paris: Flammarion, 1991.

Virilio, P., *The Art of the Motor*, trans. J. Rose. Minneapolis: University of Minnesota Press, 1995. Originally publ. as *L'art du moteur*, Paris: Galilée, 1993.

Virilio, P., *Open Sky*, trans. J. Rose. London: Verso, 2000. Originally publ. as *La vitesse de libération*, Paris: Galilée, 1995.

Weber, A., *History of Philosophy* (1896). In A. Weber and R. B. Perry, *History of Philosophy, with Philosophy since 1860*, New York: Charles Scribner's Sons, 1925, pp. 1–457.

Weber, M., *The Protestant Ethic and the Spirit of Capitalism* (1904–5), trans. T. Parsons, introd. A. Giddens. London: Unwin Hyman, 1989.

Wells, H. G., *The Time Machine* (1895). London: Pan Books, 1980.

Whitehead, A. N., *An Enquiry Concerning Principles of Natural Knowledge*. Cambridge: Cambridge University Press, 1919.

Whitehead, A. N., *Process and Reality*. New York: Harper & Row, 1929.

Whitelegg, J., *Transport for a Sustainable Future: The Case for Europe*. London: Belhaven Press, 1993.

Whitelegg, J., *Critical Mass: Transport, Environment and Society in the Twenty-First Century*. London: Pluto Press, 1997.

Whitrow, G. J., *Time in History: The Evolution of our General Awareness of Time and Temporal Perspective*. Oxford: Oxford University Press, 1988.

Whorf, B. L., *Language, Thought and Reality*. Cambridge: MIT Press, 1956.

Wood, J., *The Celtic Book of Living and Dying*. London: Duncan Baird, 2000.

Zerubavel, E., *Hidden Rhythms: Schedules and Calendars in Social Life*. Chicago: University of Chicago Press, 1981.

Zerubavel, E., *The Seven Day Cycle: The History and Meaning of the Week*. Chicago: University of Chicago Press, 1985.

Zohar, D., *Through the Time Barrier*. London: Paladin, 1983.

Index

a priori knowledge *see*
  knowledge
action: Schutz on 67–9
African mythology 154–5*n*
agriculture 88; genotechnology
  142; technical control
  96–7
Albrow, M. 44
Anaxagoras 25, 63
Anne, Queen 118
anthropology: structure and
  number 93–4
Apaches 9
archaeology 93, 160*n*;
  Neanderthal burials 92; time
  reckoning 104–5
Aristotle: form and measure of
  motion 27–9; Newton and
  29; *Physics* 28
art and architecture: ancient
  megalithic temples 80–1;
  arresting time 79–81
Assmann, Jan 84
astronomical bodies: calendars
  and 109–11; cycles of
  105–8; mythology of cycles
  6; rhythms of 99

Augustine, Saint 157*n*; *The
  City of God* 53; *Confessions*
  52, 53; consciousness of time
  52–4; later influence 57, 65;
  past/present/future 69;
  Plotinus and 51
Australian Aborigines: arresting
  time 77; dream time 9,
  154*n*
Aztecs 105, 107; mythology 7,
  14–15

Babylonia 110; mythology 15;
  reckoning time 104–5, 107
Barrett, J. 91
Bauman, Zygmunt 132–3
Beck, Ulrich 136, 147
Becker, Ernest: *The Denial of
  Death* 72
Becker, Gary 139–40
being and becoming *see*
  existence
Being and Time (Heidegger)
  57–9
Bergson, Henri 30, 55–6;
  Heidegger and 58; Mead
  and 65

Big Bang theory 10–11
birth and fertility 14–15
Bohr, Niels 62
Bolzmann, Ludwig Eduard 31
Book of the Dead 84
Bradley, R. 91
Britain: global clock-time 117;
    Neolithic 107
Buddhism 90–1
burials *see* death and decay;
    funeral rites

calendars 103, 104;
    astronomical cycles 109–11;
    first cultures and 107–8;
    Mayan 108–9; revolutionary
    111; sacred and profane time
    110–11
Capital (Marx) 38, 39
capitalism: clock-time and
    113–14; production 128–9;
    relation to future 141
Capra, Fritjof 63
Castells, Manuel: *The Rise of
    the Network Society* 134–5
causality: Aristotle on 27;
    foretelling and 87
Celtic culture 7 *see also* Druids
change 74; Aristotle on 28;
    beliefs and 91; Marx's
    perspective 40
China: the calendar 111;
    clock-time and 113, 114–15;
    heavenly cycles 6; *I Ching*/
    Book of Changes 86;
    reckoning time 104–5, 107
Christianity 90, 91;
    commodified time 125–6;
    creation 10; resurrection
    16–17; Weber on 'Protestant
    ethic' 41–5
classification 144
clock-time 44, 49, 66, 70, 101;
    colonization and 136–9;
    control and 145–7;
    creation of 112–17;

cultural differences 112–13,
    114–15; nature to mechanics
    113–16; social relations and
    127–8; speed and 128;
    transmitted time signals 119
Cohen, John 82
coincidence 8, 87
colonization 124; clock-time
    and 136–9; economics of
    139–41; other cultures
    136–8; science and the future
    141–2
communication: instantaneity
    119–21, 131–3
compression 124; economics of
    128–9; technology and
    130–8
*The Condition of
    Postmodernity* (Harvey) 125
consciousness 67–9
*A Contemporary Critique of
    Historical Materialism*
    (Giddens) 124–5
control 124; technology and
    145–7; timescapes and
    143–5
cosmology 110
creation: Big Bang theory
    10–11; mythology 7–11
Critchlow, Keith 80–1, 94
The Critique of Pure Reason
    (Kant) 34–5
culture: clock-time and
    112–13; practices 71–2;
    rhythms of 94–8
cycles 74; archaic societies
    75–6; death and 98–100;
    heavenly 105–8; knowledge
    and 102; of life in society
    98–9; reckoning time 104–5
    see also rhythm

Dante Alighieri: *Divine
    Comedy* 13–14
death and decay 74; burial and
    rituals of 89–90, 92, 93–4;

cycles and 98–100; fear of
72, 152; mythology and
12–13 *see also* immortality
Delphic oracle 85
Democritus 25–6, 63
Denbigh, K. G. 31
The Denial of Death (Becker)
72
Divine Comedy (Dante)
13–14
dreams: Aboriginal dream time
9, 154*n*; conceptions of 19
Dreyfus, H. L. 55
dromological law 131
Druids 85–6
Durkheim, Émile 22, 157*n*; on
calendars 107; *Elementary
Forms of Religious Life* 46,
103; Plato's influence 27;
social theory 36–7; social
time 45–9

economics: compression of
time 128–36; inequalities
127, 131; labour time
38–40, 126–7; time as
resource 41–5, 139–40
education 116
Egypt 83; Book of the Dead
84; mythology of 6–7, 7,
12–13, 77, 92–4, 153*n*;
reckoning time 104–6, 107;
seasons 110
Einstein, Albert: relativity
theories 61–2
*The Elementary Forms of
Religious Life* (Durkheim)
46, 103
Eliade, Mircea 77, 97, 159*n*
Elias, Norbert 104
energy: entropy 29;
thermodynamics and 31–3
Enlightenment thought 33–4
see also Hegel, Georg W. F.;
Kant, Immanuel
The Enneads (Plotinus) 51–2

environment: economic analysis
and 135; prediction and
87–9; social sciences and
131
epistemology: Husserl on 57
see also knowledge
eternity: structure and
numbers 93–4 *see also*
immortality
events: capturing performance
79
existence: fear of non- 72;
Kierkegaard on 54–5
experience 69; knowledge and
47

Fabian, Johannes 151
fate and foretelling 149; Greek
oracles 85; history of
divination 82–7; science and
technology 87–9; use of past
140
food preservation 96
Fordism 128
France 104; revolutionary
calendar 111, 112
Franklin, Benjamin 44, 126;
time is money 41–2
funeral rites 89–90, 92, 93–4;
of Neanderthals 92
future *see* fate and foretelling;
past/present/future

Game, Ann 55–6
Genesis, Book of 10
Gennep, Arnold van 98–9
genotechnology 96–7, 142,
145–6, 147
geographical time 117–19
George III, King 118
Geronimo 9
Giddens, Anthony 141; *A
Contemporary Critique of
Historical Materialism*
124–5
Gilgamesh, Epic of 12

globalization: of clock-time 117–19; instant communication 119–21; time signals 118–19; Westernized time systems 111–12

Gosden, Christopher 71, 75, 91

Greece: mathematics 93; mythology 7–8, 15–16; oracles 85; philosophy and time 23–9

Green, M. 91

Greenwich Mean Time (GMT) 117

Grundrisse (Marx) 38

Harrison, John 118

Harvey, David 128; *The Condition of Postmodernity* 125

Hassan, Robert 135–6

Hegel, Georg W. F. 23; dialectical reasoning 35–6; eternal time 36; Marx and 37; Newton's influence on 30; ontology 36; *Phenomenology of Mind* 36; *Philosophy of Nature* 36; religio-cultural change 44

Heidegger, Martin 69, 71; *Being and Time* 57–9; fear of non-existence 72

Heisenberg, Werner 62, 63–4

hell *see* other worlds

Heraclitus 24–5, 36

Hidden Rhythms (Zerubavel) 108

Hinduism 6, 7; 'Churning of the Ocean of Milk' 16; Moksha 90

history: Durkheim on 47–8; Marxism and 40–1

Homer: *The Odyssey* 13

Howard, T. 131

Hubert, H. 157*n*

Husserl, Edmund 65, 66, 69; Heidegger and 58; living present 56–7; *The Phenomenology of Internal Time Consciousness* 57

I Ching/Book of Changes 86

Icelandic mythology 9–10

immortality 123; burial of dead and 89–90, 92, 93–4; fear of death 152; knowledge and 19; resurrection 13, 16–17, 77, 92; science and 147

Incas 105

India: arresting time 77; mythology 153*n*; reckoning time 104–5, 107; time stories 6, 7, 16

industry: colonizing with time 137–8; time control and 123, 143–5 *see also* capitalism

instantaneity/simultaneity 103, 146; communication and 119–21, 131–3, 135

institutions 1

International Meridian Conference 117

Inuit moon spirit 6

Islam 90, 91; non-mechanical time 113, 115

Japan: Westernizing time 137

Jews and Judaism 90, 91, 163*n*; creation 10; fate and foretelling 83; prayer time 115; rhythms of life 108

John, Gospel of 10

Jung, Carl Gustav 86, 160*n*

Kant, Immanuel: *The Critique of Pure Reason* 34–5; Newton's influence on 30;

noumenon 35; *a priori*
knowledge 45–6; religio-
cultural changes 44
Kern, Stephen 119, 129, 138
Kierkegaard, Søren 51, 57–8,
65
knowledge: eternal life and 19;
experiential 47; external
representations 79–81; the
future and 142; Heidegger's
Being 58; information
processing 132; know-how
102–3; perception of time
66; as political endeavour
152; *a priori* 33–5, 45,
55–6; transcendent 47, 70

labour: commodified time and
38–41, 126–7
Landes, David 111, 113, 115
Le Goff, Jacques 125–6
Le Roy, Pierre 118
Lévi-Strauss, Claude: *The
Savage Mind* 77
literature 1; narrative rhythm
97–8; other worlds and
13–14 *see also* mythology
Lockyer, Sir J. Norman 105
Longitude Act 118
Longitude (Sobel) 118
luck: deities of 8; Mayan
calendars and 109

Maori mythology 9
Marconi, Guglielmo 119–20
Marinetti, Filippo Tommaso
129–30
Marx, Karl 22, 128; *Capital*
38, 39, 124; change and 40;
commodified labour-time
38–41, 124–5; *Grundrisse*
38, 124; Hegel and 36, 37;
historical time 40–1; Plato's
influence 27; social theory
36–7

mathematics: as ritual 93–4;
structure and number 93–4
Mauss, Marcel 157n
Maxwell, James Clark 119
Mayans 105, 107; calendar of
108–9
Mbiti, John 93
Mead, George Herbert 22,
53–4; *The Philosophy of the
Present* 64–6; Whitehead
and 60
medical technology:
transplantation 130, 133–4
Melbin, Murray 138
Merlin 85–6
Mesopotamian mythology 8–9
motion: Aristotle on 27–9;
atoms in 25–6; Einstein's
relativity 61–2; quantum
physics and 63; time and
51–3
Mumford, Lewis 111, 112,
114, 115
Murphy, Raymond 164n
music: performance of 79,
165n; rhythm and 97
mythology 1; arresting time
77–9; contemporary meaning
and 17–20; controlling time
146; creation 7–11; death
and resurrection 12–13, 13,
16–17; earthly cycles 6–7;
Egyptian 84, 92; Eliade on
159n; fear of death and 152;
heavenly cycles 6; of
moments 8; paradise and
loss 11, 18; renewal and
regeneration 14–16, 18; of
time stories 4 *see also*
literature

Native Americans: Apache
creation myth 9
nature: clocks and 113 *see also*
astronomical bodies

Newton, Isaac: Aristotle and
    29; clockwork universe
    29–31; overturned 31–3,
    60–1, 63; *The Principia* 29
Norse mythology 12, 160*n*
Nostradamus 83
noumena 49; Aristotle on 29;
    Kant and 35; Plato's 26–7;
    Whitehead and 60
Nowotny, Helga 142
nuclear power 88–9, 147

The Odyssey (Homer) 13
ontology: Greek thought 23–4;
    Hegel on 36
other worlds: Egyptian Book of
    the Dead 84; fear of death
    and 72; myth and literature
    5–6, 13–14, 15–16; Plato's
    noumena 19, 26–7

paradise 11, 18
paradox of Zeno 24
Parmenides 24, 25, 65
past/present/future 149;
    colonization of 140–3;
    existence and becoming
    54–60; historical sense
    150–1; Mead on 64–6;
    social theory 69; St
    Augustine on 53–4 *see also*
    fate and foretelling
permanence: beliefs and 89–94
    see also immortality
Perry, R. B. 56–7
phenomenology: Husserl 56–7;
    Schutz and 66–9
*The Phenomenology of
    Internal Time Consciousness*
    (Husserl) 57
Phenomenology of Mind
    (Hegel) 36
phenomenon 35
Philosophy of Nature (Hegel)
    36

The Philosophy of the Present
    (Mead) 64–6
Plato 35; numbers and
    geometry 93, 94; theory of
    ideas/*noumena* 19, 26–7, 60
Plotinus: *The Enneads* 51–2
politics 139
Poster, Mark 146
power relations 1
prediction *see* fate and
    foretelling
Prigogine, Ilya: dissipative
    structures 32–3
The Principia (Newton) 29
*The Protestant Ethic and the
    Spirit of Capitalism* (Weber)
    41–5
Pythagoras 94, 106

quantum physics 62–4, 160*n*

reality: time as expression of
    59–60
Reanney, D. 20, 76
reason: *a priori* knowledge
    and 34–5; dialectical 35–6,
    37
reckoning *see* calendars;
    clock-time
religion and belief systems:
    ancient concepts 3–4; change
    91; Durkheim on 45–6;
    immortality and permanence
    89–94; prayer time 115
resurrection *see* immortality
rhythm: clock-time and society
    116; counting time and 103;
    modifying 94–8; music and
    literature 97–8
Richard II the Lionheart
    85–6
Rifkin, Jeremy 131; *Time Wars*
    128
*The Rise of the Network
    Society* (Castells) 134–5

ritual: arresting time 77–9; life cycles and 98–9; technology replaces need for 138

Russia: revolutionary calendar 111, 112; Westernizing time 137

sacred and profane time 108; calendars and 110–11

The Savage Mind (Lévi-Strauss) 77

Schutz, Alfred 22, 53–4, 66–9; *The Problem of Social Reality* 67

science 139; atoms in motion 25–6; Big Bang theory 10–11; colonization of future 141–2; Einstein's relativity 61–2; Newton overturned 60–1, 63; Newton's clockwork universe 29–31; prediction 87–9; Prigogine's dissipative structures 32–3; quantum physics 62–4, 160n; space-time 56; thermodynamics and energy 31–3

Serres, Michel 144

Sharp, Clifford 139–40

shipping 118

Sobel, Dava: *Longitude* 118

social science theory 1–2; constructivism 47–8; context of concepts 150–3; Durkheim's social time 45–9; engagement in time 22–3; environment and 131; Mead's past/present/future 64–6; from ontology to practice 36–7; as political endeavour 152; Weber on economics of time 41–5

society 1, 101; archaic 75–6; rhythms of 99, 116;

structures of 71–2; transplants and 130

soul/spirit: defining 155n; Greek thought 26; Kierkegaard on existence 54–5

space-time 55–6

Standard Railway Time 117

Su Sung 113

Sumeria 107

Taoism 86, 90, 91

Taylorism 128

technology 2; agriculture 96–7; clocks 112–13, 118–19; communication 119–21, 131–3; compression and 130–8; conquest of cold and dark 138; control of time with 145–7; cultural effects 73; fire and daily rhythms 95–6; genetic 142, 145–6, 147; information processing 132–3; scientific prediction and 87–9; transplants 133–4; transport 130–1

telegraphy 119–20

thermodynamics, laws of 31–3

Thom, Alexander 106

Thompson, E. P. 29; 'Time, Work-Discipline and Industrial Capitalism' 113–14

time: absolute 30–1; arresting 77–81; categorizing relations 151–2; colonization 136–43; commodified 38–41, 139–40; complexities and hierarchies 122; compressions 128–36; control with 143–8; controlling 121, 123–4; defining 3–5, 21, 50; as eternal 36; linear 75–6;

time (*cont'd*)
  multiple expressions of 1–2;
  reckoning 103–12;
  representation and 79–81;
  space and 55–6;
  transcendence 74 *see also*
  calendars; clock-time;
  rhythm
The Time Machine (Wells) 129
time travel 129
Time Wars (Rifkin) 128
timescapes 143–5
transcendence 74, 143, 152;
  immortality and 147;
  knowledge and 47, 70
transience 74
transplants 133–4, 146
travel and transport:
  compression of 130–1;
  controlling time 146;
  standard global time 117–19

Virilio, Paul: 'From Superman
  to Hyperactive Man' 133–4;
  technological compression
  130–4

Weber, Alfred 34–5
Weber, Max 22, 124; Plato's
  influence 27; *The Protestant
  Ethic and the Spirit of
  Capitalism* 41–5; Schutz and
  66; social theory 36–7; time
  as a resource 41–5, 115, 125
Wells, H. G.: *The Time
  Machine* 129
Whitehead, Alfred North:
  Mead and 65; time as
  expression of reality 59–60

Zeno of Elea: paradox of 24
Zerubavel, Eviator 107;
  Hidden Rhythms 108